JOYRIDE

A MEMOIR

LARRY E. HILL

Joyride: A Memoir
Copyright © 2024 by Larry E. Hill
All rights reserved.

ISBN: 979-8-218-39901-6 (paperback)
ISBN: 979-8-218-39902-3 (hardcover)

Book Design: Kelly Nielsen, Studio92.us

Printed in the United States of America

DEDICATION

I dedicate this book to my loving wife, Jill, and daughters, Allison and Emily.

Jill because she not only encouraged me to write the book, but she was hands-on throughout the entire process. She frequently researched things for me and wrote much of the book herself. She has a lot of time invested in this project. In addition, she puts up with me, which is not easy.

There would not have been a book without Allison and Emily. They have been the joy of my life for over thirty years. Both have asked for years, "Dad, would you write a book about your life?" They are two great young ladies. My mother and dad would have been proud of them.

I love you all.

TABLE OF CONTENTS

INTRODUCTION

THE TURNING POINT

It's 1977, and I'm twenty-one years old. I've been working out of an old shop, painting and repairing beaten-up junk cars. I'm renting the building from a local attorney and the equipment from a guy named Ray.

I've gotten myself in a little deep—and quickly. I keep wondering if I'm going to make it. I'm worried that I will never be able to scratch out a living. Will I even have the money to pay the $155 rent on my furnished duplex? I've been determined to make it work, but now I'm not sure I can.

While sitting in my recliner late one night, a heavy cloud of doubt, worry, and fear consumes my thoughts. The more anxious I get, the more defeated I feel, and the more defeated I feel, the more anxious I get. It's a vicious loop.

For some reason, my attention turns to a box I had packed when I was leaving Raleigh a few months back to move to Florida. In it are a few incidentals I had lying around, including a couple of books. I've had one of the books since high school, but I've never read even a page of it.

When I was seventeen, having trouble in high school, I spent my fair share of time in the principal's office. One day while there for getting into trouble yet again, the principal handed me a book and said, "Larry, I want you to read this." It was Dr. Norman Vincent Peale's book, *The Power of Positive Thinking: A Practical Guide to Mastering the Problems of Everyday Living.* I took the book and walked out. I guess I didn't pass a trash can between his office and my classroom or I would've thrown it away. Somehow, that book made it back to my parents' house that day, and then it made it to Florida with me in that box years later.

I start reading the book. It is so compelling and uplifting that I keep reading until one or two o'clock in the morning, falling asleep in my recliner.

In the beginning of the book, Dr. Peale writes that he had just spoken at a convention when a guy walked up to him and said, "May I talk with you about a matter of desperate importance to me?"

Dr. Peale asked him to remain until the other people had left, and then he sat down backstage with the man, who explained that he was in town to handle the most important business deal of his life. If he failed, he said he would be "done for." The forty-year-old man explained that he had been tormented by a lack of confidence his entire life. He said he listened to Dr. Peale's presentation and wanted to know how he could build faith in himself.

After telling the man it would take some time and analysis to get to the root of his issues, Dr. Peale told him he did have a formula to use right away. He told the man to keep repeating to himself, "I can do all things through Christ who strengthens me"—upon waking, throughout the day, and before bed. The man followed this advice, and it did wonders for him. He also sought counseling and overcame his feeling of inferiority.[1]

Dr. Peale's belief, and one of the main points in his book, is that when we consciously replace negative thoughts with positive ones, we become happier and more successful. When we look to God to sustain us, we no longer need to worry.

The next morning, I wake up and drive to my auto body shop. I am intrigued by the power of Dr. Peale's book. I'm all by myself in the shop that morning, as usual, painting a customer's Volkswagen Beetle. All of a sudden, I start crying like a baby. This is unsettling because I'm not an emotional person. I never have been. Remembering Dr. Peale's advice to the guy who had approached him, I start repeating Philippians 4:13 from the Bible: "I can do all things through Christ who strengthens me. I can do all things through Christ who strengthens me." I continue repeating it.

I must have said it two hundred times while painting that car.

I've got to tell you, when I walked out of the shop that day, something had changed. I was a bit of a different person.

1. Dr. Norman Vincent Peale, *The Power of Positive Thinking: A Practical Guide to Mastering the Problems of Everyday Living* (New York: Simon & Schuster, 1952, 1956, 1980), 1–3.

I had a better outlook on my future. I felt different. I didn't feel the anxiety and fear I'd had for so long.

After that, things started taking a turn for the better in my life. I changed the way I thought. When a negative or pessimistic thought snuck into my head, I slapped it down by repeating Philippians 4:13. The more positive my thoughts became, the more success I experienced, and the less fear I felt.

The book made such an impact on my life that over the years, I have bought fifty or more copies and given them to people who I felt could benefit from the book. Below is the quote from the book that I most took to heart:

"The secret of a better and more successful life is to cast out those old, dead, unhealthy thoughts. Substitute for them new, vital, dynamic faith thoughts. You can depend upon it—an inflow of new thought will remake you and your life."

—Dr. Norman Vincent Peale,
The Power of Positive Thinking

When I first began thinking about writing my life story, it felt a little odd because I've never been much of a "memories" guy. I have rarely looked back at situations in my life. I've always preferred to look forward. I think that's because for much of my life, I was not happy with the present. I was always looking for a brighter future, waiting for the present to be over and behind me. I didn't want to record what was happening at the time.

What inspired me to write this book was having grandchildren. It is an unrivaled blessing. My grandkids call me "Pop." One day, while holding baby Luca in my arms, it occurred to me that he sees me only as his loving, adoring, doting grandfather. He and my other grandchildren will never know much about my life—my career, my successes, my failures, and the challenges I've overcome—unless I share my story with them.

As of September 2023, Jill and I had six grandchildren. My younger daughter has two children, Jill's middle daughter has two, and her son has twin boys. They are all younger than six years old. Some of their earliest memories will be about "Birdie and Pop." They will remember our fun times in the sun, living in Florida most of the year and living on Lookout Mountain, Tennessee, a suburb of Chattanooga, part of the year.

By the time our grandkids were born, I had already retired. When they grow up, they will know I was a new-car dealer, but they won't know many details about my childhood, my career, or my work ethic and values. My daughters, Allison and Emily, don't know parts of my life and career, either—especially about my early days, before I met their mom, Gayle.

After my parents passed away, I often wished I had known more about their lives. These are things we don't think about until it's too late. I don't want my children and grandchildren wondering what my life was like— or what I was really like. I wrote this memoir for them. I want to tell my story so my children, stepchildren, and grandchildren know who I am: a student of people, life, and the car business—not just a dad and "Pop." I want them to know the good, the bad, and the other—how I grew up, how my upbringing shaped my worldview, and how I overcame the tough times.

I also want them to know what I've learned about other people overcoming adversity and

Emily's son, Luca, and me ("Pop"), in 2019.

discovering how they pulled through when they felt their backs were against the wall. This has always given me inspiration and resolve. I've always enjoyed reading stories about people who toughed it out when things got hard instead of giving up.

Although I've experienced many ups and downs, it has been an exciting and fulfilling journey. I've made a lot of mistakes, but I've also made decisions that brought great joy and success. Knowing God is in control has been liberating. It has freed me from the constant responsibility of trying to orchestrate outcomes. Before learning this lesson, worry robbed me of the joy of life.

A *joyride* is a trip taken for pleasure. Life should have more joyrides than burdens, yet it's impossible to appreciate them when you're worried about what might lie in the road ahead. The key is to let the worry go and enjoy the ride.

Read on, and you'll see what I mean.

The mantra that inspires me every day is, "Winners never quit. Quitters never win." This quote is from Vince Lombardi (1913–70), who many people consider not just the greatest coach in football history, but also one of the greatest coaches and leaders in our history. When he was the head coach of the Green Bay Packers during the 1960s, he led the team to three straight and five total NFL Championships in seven years.

The rock pictured below sits on my desk in my study. I bought it thirty-five years ago. Every day, it reminds me of my mission, which is to make the most of what God has given me.

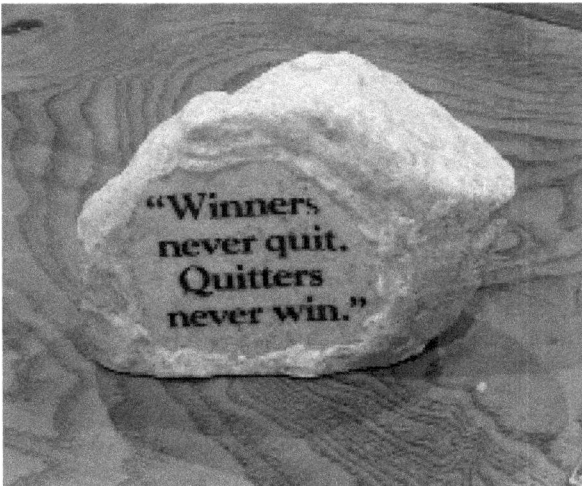

The mantra that has inspired me for more than thirty years, engraved on a rock that sits on my desk.

1

MY MOSTLY IDYLLIC CHILDHOOD IN NORTH CAROLINA

I was born on March 28, 1956, to Ernest and Rometa Hill at Rex Hospital in Raleigh, North Carolina. I have two sisters— Linda, who is eight years older than me, and Susan, who was three years older than me. For my first seven years, we lived in a little house at 1705 Patton Road in Raleigh. Ours was a small home with three bedrooms in a middle-class neighborhood. It may have been built as a two-bedroom, with one room converted to a third bedroom for me. Linda and Susan shared a room, Mom and Dad had a room, and I had a small room. The house also had one bathroom, along with the kitchen, the dining room, and a small living room. That was it. This was typical of the houses in the neighborhood.

Living in a small neighborhood, in a small house, on a small lot in Raleigh felt foreign to Dad. I think he always yearned to get back to where there was a little space and land, similar to where he had been raised. He didn't necessarily want a farm, but he longed to have a little property. That was part of his identity, and it was familiar to him.

My first memories begin when I was four, Linda was twelve, and Susan was seven. I spent the days at home with Mom while my sisters were in school. She didn't work outside our home at that time, so most of the activities I did were with her. When she ran errands, I would go with her.

We often went to the grocery store. Back then, stores gave out stamps as an incentive, or loyalty, program. The two types of stamps were S&H Green Stamps and Gold Bond Stamps. When we went to pay, depending on how much we were spending, the cashier would rip off a few pages of stamps and hand them to my mother. We had stamp books at the house, so we'd go home, lick the stamps, and put them in the books. When the books were full of stamps, we'd take them to the "redemption" centers and exchange them for merchandise—an iron, a toaster, or something else my mother needed for the house. This errand was bearable for a young boy, and even fun, because of the stamps.

The errand I dreaded most was going to the fabric stores with Mom. She sewed clothes for my two sisters and herself. I vividly recall these trips because I disliked them so much! There was nothing for me to do, and Mom could drag it out for hours. That's an eternity for a kid who's in an environment he doesn't like. I'd just wander around, trying to find something to do. I usually ended up sitting in a corner on the floor or under a table among some of the bolts of fabric, just waiting for her to finish.

While I spent the days with Mom, my father was busy at Capital Paint and Wallpaper Company. He was co-owner along with his partner, Buddy Clement. They met when they were house painters at different companies, and then a couple of years or so before I was born, they started their own business together.

A few other memories come to mind. When I was probably four, I liked to open the front door and sit on the floor. I'd look out the glass storm door and wait for the garbage men to come. I loved watching the big truck come squealing up the street, the guys dumping bins of trash in the back and then hitting those levers. The truck would gobble up all the trash and then squeal off again. I used to think that was the coolest thing in the world. For a long time, I wanted to be a garbage man. I see the sanitation company picking up our bins today and think of those early years. I don't think the technology on garbage trucks has changed much in sixty years.

We had milkmen who delivered fresh milk to people's homes during these years. We would set a small metal cooler on the front porch. The milkman would come by in the morning in a truck. The back was filled with a huge mound of shaved ice, with milk bottles sitting in the ice to keep them cool. He would stop at the house and place however many bottles of milk we had ordered in the milk box. In the summer when we were out of school, we'd run behind the milkman's truck. When he would open the back of the truck to get the milk bottles, we'd all reach in there, grab a handful of the shaved ice and eat it. He'd let us do this for a minute or two before driving on to his next stop.

I had a couple of friends nearby. Lynn Gosnell lived next door. She was about a year younger than me, and we became close friends. As a matter of fact, I think Lynn was kind of like my first "girlfriend." We hung out quite a bit together, usually at her house with her mom.

Most of the kids in our neighborhood were boys, except for Lynn. We would ride our bikes and play in the street. Eric Dean lived across the street, and his parents were good friends with mine. He was a couple of years older than me. Other than doing some stuff in the summer or riding bikes after school, we didn't hang out a whole lot.

My best Christmas ever was the year I got two big gifts—a bicycle and a sled. We usually got one big gift and a few small ones, but I made out like a bandit that year. I couldn't believe it! I had to do a double take when I went in the living room and saw my gifts. There I was at the age of five with not one, but two, modes of transportation. How about that?

We typically had some snow every year in Raleigh. After I got my sled, I would get very excited when it snowed. Not only would school be canceled for a day or two, but I also had endless hours of fun all bundled up in my coat and mittens, riding that sled down the nearby hills.

The road next to the Deans' house was a big hill, and the top of the hill intersected with our street. It then went straight down and ran into a pretty busy road. At that time, it was a two-lane road. One day, it started snowing late in the day. By the time it got dark, the snow was really piling up. There was a full moon, or close to it, so it was pretty bright outside for that time of night. Ten or so of us kids were out there with our sleds, sliding down the hill by the Deans' house. A couple of the parents hung out down at the bottom just to make sure we didn't get carried away and slide into the road. We'd race our sleds down the hill and crash at the bottom, having a big time. We'd pull the sleds back up the hill and do it again. Those are some of the best times I recall having as a child.

On Sundays, our family went to Sunday school and church at Emmanuel Baptist Church. I had one of those gray suits made of wool, and it didn't have a lining. It was itchy, as if made of burlap. I was kind of finicky already about itchy stuff, and that suit just drove me crazy. I didn't mind going to Sunday school and church, but I dreaded putting on that suit. Somehow, as did the other boys back then, I survived.

After Sunday school, everyone would meet under the porte-cochere that was between the sanctuary and the other buildings at the church. The men, including my dad, would be out there smoking cigarettes and talking. After a few minutes, we'd gather and head into the sanctuary to hear the sermon from our pastor, L. D. Holt.

On occasion, maybe once a month or so, Mom and Dad would decide that after Sunday school we would drive to Grandma's house. We would go to Sunday school and then skip "big church," as we called it, and I would get out of that wool suit earlier than usual! These two things tickled me to death.

Grandma Hill lived in the small town of Salemburg, North Carolina, the area where my parents were raised. It was about an hour's drive from Raleigh. As a young boy, it seemed the trip always took longer than an hour while riding in the backseat down the two-lane rural roads of North Carolina.

I don't know how Grandma knew when we were coming to visit because she didn't have a telephone. Dad's youngest brother had a phone, so maybe Dad would call him. There were fifteen children in my father's family, all within twenty years of each other, and the oldest and the youngest sons both lived next door to each other, across the street from Grandma as adults. One of them could have walked across the street to let her know.

She would have a big dinner cooked and ready for us to eat. We called the midday meal "dinner" in the South. The evening meal was "supper." I didn't hear the word "lunch" until I was twenty-one years old and living in Florida! Man, she'd have a big spread. Grandma raised chickens, so we'd often have fried chicken with collard or turnip greens and homemade biscuits. She would go out in the mornings before we arrived and wring the necks of one or two chickens, pluck the feathers, clean the birds, and then start frying.

Due to the number of children Grandma Hill had, there were always tons of aunts, uncles, and cousins nearby who would come to visit. Uncle Merty, the second-oldest child, had a little general store at the end of Grandma's street. The adults would give us a couple of nickels or dimes and let us walk to Merty's store to get a candy bar or Coke. Later in the afternoon, my parents, my sisters, and I would head back to Raleigh.

Grandpa Hill had passed away when I was around five years old, but I do have earlier memories of him. He was in a wheelchair, having had both legs amputated due to diabetes. In any event, it didn't seem to bother him. Grandma and Grandpa couldn't travel, so I only saw Grandpa at their home. He was either in the kitchen, in the sitting area, on the back porch, or in the backyard. They had a ramp built from the porch to the backyard so he could roll the wheelchair outside where the chicken coop was located. He navigated pretty well, and I remember him being a happy, jovial, and funny guy with a good attitude. He was active and always dressed nicely, rolling himself around in the wheelchair and smoking cigarettes he had rolled himself. If he rolled one in front of me, he'd let me light it for him. Another highlight!

I had what I would consider a normal childhood until I was about seven years old. When we lived on Patton Road, I had a lot of friends in the neighborhood and a lot of fun. I had everything I needed—but that was about to change.

When I was seven, we moved from Patton Road to Lead Mine Road. Mom and Dad had bought an old house with two acres of property. It was three or four miles outside the Raleigh city limits, and we referred to it as being "out in the country." With the move, Dad had given in to his desire to own a little bit of land. I lived there until I left home at the age of twenty-one. It was a miserable experience. I was lonely, isolated, and bored. I especially dreaded the summers, which was so unlike a typical kid.

I was going into second grade at the time and had to change schools. I transferred to Effie Green Elementary School, part of the Wake County School System. When we lived on Patton Road, my school was J. Y. Joyner, a Raleigh city school. Our mailing address was still in Raleigh, but we had moved out of the boundaries of the city limits, and I officially became a county-school student.

County schools always had a stigma of not being as good as city schools. For one reason, city schools received funding from the county and the city, while county schools got funding from the county only. You automatically had a little bit of a black eye if you told someone, "Oh, I go to Millbrook High School" because everyone knew it was a county school. It was more prestigious if you said you went to Broughton or Sanderson or Carroll because they were all city schools.

That move wasn't good for me. Not only was I now in the inferior county school system, I also no longer had my neighborhood friends.

Some of the kids I went to school with lived in remote areas like we did, but most lived in neighborhoods that were zoned for my school. Occasionally my friends would invite me to go home with them after school to attend birthday parties, sleepovers, and other events.

They were typical middle-class, middle-income type neighborhoods. Everybody's dad worked, and all the moms seemed to stay at home and take care of the kids. I liked going to other kids' houses after school. We'd get a snack and then go outside to play or ride our bikes. It was a great environment. I could immediately feel the difference—going from the energy and camaraderie in those neighborhoods to being isolated out on Lead Mine Road. It was really depressing. I'm not sure at the time I knew it was depressing, but it was. From time to time, I would have someone over for a sleepover, but it was never really a lot of fun because it'd be only me and one other person out there in the middle of nowhere. There was only so much we could do. It was a lot more fun going to someone else's house than having them to our house. I longed for the days at Patton Road.

I played Little League baseball for Pepsi-Cola for two years while in elementary school. Mom and Dad would go to the games because they took place in the evenings in the summer, which was Dad's downtime. Other times when I played sports, if a game was on a Saturday morning or on a weekday afternoon, my parents didn't attend. Dad was working, and he wasn't going to stop working to go watch any kind of game because sports weren't really on his radar. All he knew was work. They didn't tell me I couldn't play sports; they just didn't encourage me. There really wasn't a lot of room in their world for play.

At the time of our move, Susan was ten, and Linda was fifteen. Susan and I would hang out some, but I didn't spend much time with Linda. Being eight years apart and of different genders, we didn't have much in common. I'm sure both my sisters felt just as bored and isolated as I did. However, Dad liked it there. He was a workaholic. He would get up in the mornings and go to work at his paint store. He was a good businessman. He typically met customers at their houses to give them painting quotes, while Mr. Clement spent more time in the retail store.

I think Dad was a better communicator. He was easy to talk to and well-spoken. He could talk to anyone, whether it was his painters, a doctor, a judge, or any of his customers.

He painted a lot of large homes in those historical areas of Raleigh. He was very engaging. He always wore dress pants and a shirt and tie to work. When he got home around 5:30 each weekday afternoon, he would change out of his dress clothes and into his work clothes. He and Mr. Clement would occasionally take turns leaving early, so some days, Dad would get home by four o'clock.

Dad always had some sort of project. The house on Lead Mine Road needed work when he and Mom purchased it. He probably had two years' worth of work the day we moved in there. I was his helper. My dad always called me Beau for some reason. I never saw it written, so I don't know if it was "Beau" or "Bo."

On weekday mornings, he would go down to Finch's Diner for coffee. It was a classic 1950s-style diner a block from his store. They knew him well. As soon as he walked in, a waitress would bring him a cup of coffee. He would drink his coffee, smoke a cigarette, and then head out to check on his jobs and go to customers' houses to give estimates. He always made sure everything was going well on the jobsites before heading back to the store.

During the summer mornings, his schedule changed somewhat. Dad would go to the shop and get his men off to work, and instead of going to Finch's, he would make the 20-to-25-minute drive back home to get his cup of coffee. He also needed to share his plan for the day with me. Before we moved, I couldn't wait for school to be over and for summer to begin. Upon getting to Land Mine Road, though, I dreaded summer because I knew I was going to be working on Dad's projects all day. Now, if something came up, like an invitation to go somewhere or attend a birthday party or other event, my parents let me go. They never told me I couldn't, but those days were few and far between.

A lot of the work Dad had me doing was in the garden. He always planted a big garden and really enjoyed taking care of it. He would take his tiller and turn the soil in the garden to get it ready for planting. This would bring up a bunch of rocks, some of which were pretty big. I tossed a lot of rocks out of that garden and pulled a lot of weeds. Dad expected me to complete a certain amount of work each day before he got home in the evenings.

Another project was the front porch. It was large and made of poured concrete, which wasn't at all uncommon for porches back then. Dad wanted to repaint it because the paint was peeling. He had a utility knife, which was a small scraper with a razor blade in it. You would push a small lever with your thumb to expose the standard-size razor blade, maybe an inch wide. He had me scrape that huge porch with that tiny blade. It took me more than a week to finish it, on my hands and knees, scraping all day. It was a miserable job. Dad wasn't trying to be cruel; it's just that work is all he knew, and he felt that because I was home all summer, I should be doing something productive. While most kids dreaded going back to school at the end of summer, I couldn't wait for school to start so I could get out of there.

Summers did include a family vacation each year. We typically alternated between the beach and the mountains. I don't remember if we kids had any input or not or if Mom and Dad always chose the location. If we went to the beach, we'd go for an entire week. Mom and Dad would rent rooms at a small motor-lodge motel or a house. That was our home base, and Mom would cook a lot. A couple of times, we'd go out to eat. We'd spend the days just hanging out at the beach. Our mountain vacations were a little different. We wouldn't stay at the same place for the entire week. We would go to various attractions, and sometimes they would be a couple of hours apart. Therefore, we moved around quite a bit to different motels. We'd go to places like Grandfather Mountain near Linville, North Carolina, and Tweetsie Railroad in Blowing Rock, North Carolina.

My mom would praise me for getting good grades, while my dad would give me accolades when I accomplished something work-related. He was tough on me if I got bad grades, though. If I came home with a bad report card, there was no counseling from him. He didn't say, "Hey, let's sit down and talk about this and see where you might be able to improve." It was, "You'd better get these grades up, or you're not going to amount to anything. You're not going to be able to make a living for yourself, and you'll end up living under a bridge somewhere."

He would say, "You're going to be sorry." He used the word "sorry" a lot.

One time, I got a "C" in conduct, and I got a spanking for it. Back in our day, when I was coming up, it was common for kids to get spankings. Dad would spank me with a belt and Mom with a switch that she would get from a tree limb outside. Mom and Dad used the tools they had to discipline me, and they were few. No one taught them how to raise kids. As time went on, I realized that my dad wasn't a good motivator. He seemed to do well with the people who worked for him, but not with me. Back then, teachers were permitted to give kids spankings, beginning in middle school. But in elementary school, the only one who gave a spanking was the principal. I guess they had to be a little more careful with the younger kids. I clearly remember on more than one occasion getting a spanking from the principal.

When I got into middle school, every teacher had a paddle hanging in the classroom. Some teachers went to the trouble of personalizing the paddles with custom designs. These wooden paddles were about an inch thick and maybe six inches wide. Down at one end, the wood was carved into a handle for a firm grip. Often, the paddles had holes drilled in the middle. When you got hit with a paddle, it would really sting where those holes were, and it would leave a mark.

When I was twelve years old, I was "saved" at church during Vacation Bible School—I accepted Jesus Christ as my personal Savior. Having attended church with my family all my life, I understood what it meant to be a Christian at the most fundamental level, but I didn't fully embrace all it really entailed. I didn't fully learn to rely on God during my tough times until years later.

2

MEET THE HILL FAMILY

My parents were married in November 1947; I don't know the day. My mom was seventeen, and my dad was twenty-one. Mom's best friend had married Dad's brother, and the two couples shared a small apartment above a grocery store.

My mother, Rometa Cooper, was born on April 16, 1930, one of ten children born to Wiley and Mildred Cooper. Her dad was a barber. He was also an alcoholic, and he would routinely disappear for several days at a time. I don't remember him. A couple of my mother's brothers became alcoholics, as did my mother. However, I believe both brothers were sober for a good while before they passed away.

After we moved out to Lead Mine Road, Mom went to work at the Boylan-Pearce Department Store in Raleigh, in the accounting department. She had some accounting experience; how she got it, I don't remember.

Back then, most department stores were open until nine o'clock on Monday nights—later than other nights. Mom stayed late with the other workers. I looked forward to Monday nights because we got to stay up late. We didn't have to go to bed until she came home, so I'd get to watch a couple of TV shows that I normally didn't get a chance to see because they came on past my bedtime.

After that, my mother went to work for a concrete construction company, R. L. Martin Incorporated. They poured concrete for commercial jobs, and Mom ran the office. I think it was a high-stress job. My impression was that Mr. Martin wasn't a good businessman and didn't know how to manage money. Mom was always running around making sure there was enough money scraped together to make payroll and pay the bills.

Mr. Martin thought a lot of Mom. He provided her with a company car, and it was always a very nice one. He had a lot of "toys," including a motorcycle, sports cars, and vacation homes. That's probably one reason he was struggling financially.

I don't remember my mother having a drink of alcohol until I was sixteen or seventeen years old, and that was really only when we were on vacation. When I left home in early 1977, Mom and Dad lived in the house alone. I think that is probably when her alcohol consumption became more frequent. I don't know that for sure because I wasn't there, but it went from her basically never drinking when she was a mother of young children, to her drinking minimally when she was in her early forties, and on to being a full-blown alcoholic by the time she was sixty.

Mom was in her forties when she worked in the office for Mr. Martin. When they would be finishing up their workday, Mr. Martin and some of his key supervisors would go back to the office and have a cocktail before heading home. They included Mom in this ritual, and I think this was her introduction to daily cocktails.

By that time, Dad kept a little bourbon and gin in a cabinet at the house. I rarely saw him drink, but sometimes when Mom would come home stressed from pressure at work, Dad would offer her a drink. I was about seventeen, and I would hear him say, "Hey, come on in and sit down. Let me fix you a little something to calm you down." I think Mom's dependence on alcohol escalated from there.

Mom died in March 2000 at the age of sixty-nine. The cause of death was cirrhosis of the liver due to alcohol abuse. The last decade of her life was tough on her and everyone else in the family as well. The disease slowly erased the wife, mother, and grandmother we had known.

Linda took excellent care of Mom during her last few months, and when Mom passed, Linda took care of Dad. Linda was the only one left in Raleigh, so the responsibility of taking care of both our parents fell on her shoulders. I drove back as often as possible from Florida to help. Susan somewhat disappeared, beginning her own journey of substance abuse and addiction.

My father, Elmer Ernest Hill, was born on May 15, 1926, one of fifteen children, to Claude and Lou Hill (known simply as Ms. Lou). We never knew Dad's first name was

Elmer until we were older and saw it written. He had always used Ernest as his first name.

The Great Depression hit when my father was three or four years old and caused the family huge financial problems, as it did for many. My dad's father, Claude Hill, had been a successful businessman. In addition to other endeavors, he was in the lumber business. I have heard stories of the very big, almost mansion-type house where they lived. My father was the next to the youngest. The youngest of the fifteen children passed away in September 2023.

After losing the businesses, Dad's family mostly farmed, as they owned a lot of land. Because of his young age, I'm not sure he remembered the days of family wealth before the Depression.

Some of the Hill children never left Salemburg. I've never seen a town that has changed so little in the past sixty years. The last time I was there was in 2017. I'm not sure there is even a traffic light in town. It's still an extremely small community. In 2020, the population was just 461.

By the time Dad was born, some of the older siblings were leaving home or were already in the military. Like several of his brothers, after graduating from high school, Dad joined the US Army. One day in 1944, he walked out the front door of the family home to the bus "pickup spot" in Salemburg. The closest actual bus station was sixteen miles away in Clinton. He was gone for four years during World War II and spent much of that time in Italy.

When his tour of duty was over in 1948, he arrived back in New York City on a troop transport ship. He was able to spend a couple of days there and do a little sightseeing.

He loved telling the story about going to a jewelry shop and buying a new gold Longines watch. Later, he boarded a bus back to Clinton and hitchhiked home to Salemburg. Nobody knew he was out of the service until he walked back into the house!

Dad went to work for his cousin as a house painter before marrying my mother and renting the apartment above the grocery store. Shortly after, they decided to move to Raleigh. Nobody really knows why they chose to leave Salemburg. There's a good chance it was because Mom was pregnant before they got married, and they could hide it better there. Although Raleigh was only sixty miles away, there were limited travel and communication options at that time, so it was like moving across the country.

In Raleigh, Dad went to work for a paint contractor named Henry Hill (no relation). When Henry died, his wife asked Dad to run the business. He did for a few years, and later he and Buddy Clement opened Capital Paint and Wallpaper Company.

Other than those couple days in NYC on his way back home from Italy, Dad had never traveled anywhere. I don't think Mom had ever left the Salemburg area. I'm sure moving to Raleigh was a big change for them—both exciting and scary. Raleigh is the capital of North Carolina and was a large city. I'm sure glad my parents moved to Raleigh. I can't imagine growing up in a town as small as Salemburg.

As a Mason, also known as a Freemason[2], Dad was a member of the Masonic Lodge in Raleigh. It's not a "secret society," as some people think, but the members do share secret handshakes and ritual readings during their meetings. I don't know much about it. It's a tight-knit community, and they don't discuss what goes on in their meetings. When I was a little older, Dad also became a Shriner.[3]

During a typical week, Dad would come home from work, and then he and I would work on a project at the house while Mom prepared supper. We'd all sit down to eat, and then I'd do my homework. Dad would sit in his chair in the den and read his Masonic ritual book. It detailed the words and actions that Masons use during their meetings. I picked it up to read it a couple of times, and it looked like a bunch of gibberish. You had to understand the Masonic code to read it. Dad would study that little book quite a bit. He also liked to watch his favorite TV shows in the evening and smoke his cigarettes.

---

2. Freemasons belong to the oldest fraternal organization in the world, a group begun during the Middle Ages in Europe as a guild of skilled builders. See "Be a Freemason," https://beafreemason.org/masonic-life. In modern times, "Freemasons are a social and philanthropic organization. See "7 Things You May Not Know About Freemasons," History.com, https://www.history.com/news/freemasons-facts-symbols-handshake-meaning.

3. Shriners International, established in 1872, is a spin-off from Freemasonry, built on the principles that guided Freemasonry, while adding elements of fun and philanthropy that set Shriners International apart. All Shriners are Masons, but not all Masons become Shriners. See "Masons and Shriners," Calam Shriners website, https://www.calamshriners.com/what-we-do/masons-shriners-2/.

The only time Dad ever took a break from working at his job and on his projects at home was on Saturday evenings and Sundays. His wind-down time started late on Saturday afternoon. He would start relaxing with a cold beer around 3:00 or 4:00 while he was piddling in his workshop. Typically, we'd cook out on Saturday night. Dad would fire up the grill, and he'd barbecue chicken, steaks, or burgers. We never knew he had that Saturday-afternoon beer because a beer or two didn't affect him.

Dad's only real activity outside of work and projects was fishing. When we would take our family vacations at the beach, he would fish most of the time. Years later, sometimes he and I would go fishing together and we'd talk, but it wasn't a super-close relationship because our conversations were usually about work or fishing.

In the mid-1970s, as my sisters and I got older, Dad and Mom bought a little house down at Atlantic Beach in North Carolina. They enjoyed spending time there. Dad loved to fish out in the surf or from the piers. Mom liked to fish, too, but most of the time, Dad would catch the fish—typically whiting or croakers—and take them home for Mom to clean and fry. They were small fish, and she loved that she could clean them quickly.

Until I left home and went out on my own at the age of twenty-one, I had never eaten a piece of fish unless it was one my dad had caught or a fish stick in the school cafeteria. Eating fish with bones was nothing new to me because that's what I was accustomed to eating.

Dad was a smoker, and although he was moving around all the time at work, he didn't exercise. People didn't really

Joyride: Life Lessons from a Student of People, Life, and the Car Business

know about aerobic exercise back then. Plus, we ate like typical Southern people, which wasn't too healthy—fried pork chops, fried chicken, fried green tomatoes, country fried steak, fatback, eggs, bacon, and sausage. Mom made homemade biscuits for every meal unless we had spaghetti, which was once in a blue moon. When she did make spaghetti, we always had white bread with that meal.

Late one night when I was fifteen years old, Mom came into my room and said, "Hey, your dad is not feeling well. I'm going to take him to the hospital." We didn't know at the time that Dad had had a heart attack.

He was in the hospital for quite a while. When he got home, there was a long recovery period. He didn't want to stay in bed, so he wasn't getting the rest the doctors recommended.

Once Dad finally recovered, life got back to normal. He went back to smoking, but I never saw him drink much. We had a two-car garage that was connected to the house where Mom and Dad would park. We also had a little out-building that had been a garage at one time. Inside it were Dad's work tools and a refrigerator. Dad always had a six-pack of Falstaff beer in there, and he was always careful that it was obscured—wrapped up tightly in a paper bag. I don't know if I ever actually saw him drink a beer, but I knew he did occasionally because I'd open that refrigerator sometimes and look in the bag, and there would be a full six-pack in there. A few days later I would check again, and there would be one missing. They'd slowly disappear one at a time, but never on a weekday.

Years later, Dad had another heart attack, followed by open-heart surgery.

In 1985, Mom and Dad sold their home on Lead Mine Road and bought a condo in Raleigh. They enjoyed living back in town. When Mom passed away, Dad continued to live there by himself, doing his same old routine. On Sundays, he would go to church and visit with friends. On other days, he would get up in the morning, read the newspaper, watch TV, and smoke his cigarettes. There wasn't a lot to his life, but he seemed content. He met a kind, female friend at his condo development whom he enjoyed sharing time with, and I know this kept him from being lonely. Linda was there often, and I talked to him on the phone once or twice a week.

One day after Christmas in December 2004, Dad got a bad cold. He got a cold every year, maybe because he smoked so much. He was always congested and had been diagnosed with emphysema, but he wasn't on oxygen. This cold was worse than usual, so Linda took him to the hospital. His doctor wanted him to have some breathing treatments there so medical staff could keep an eye on him.

Thank goodness I was able to get there to see Dad when he was in the hospital and spend a little time with him. After I left, he was able to go home for a short period, but then he had to go back to the hospital. Dad passed away in February 2005 of congestive heart failure. For all those years, he had continued smoking but kept springing back from his heart attacks and other illnesses. I was surprised when Linda called and said, "Dad has gone to heaven." I just expected that he would spring back again. Thankfully, she had been by his side, holding his hand. The Lord always has Linda holding loved ones' hands when they pass. I was really upset that I wasn't there.

Linda was born on July 15, 1948. She is eight years older than me and five years older than Susan, the middle child, who was born on August 13, 1953.

Linda left our family home when she was around twenty years old and moved into an apartment. I remember she had a nice white 1965 Mustang Fastback—a really cool car. She worked for the state attorney general's office and then a private attorney and was doing her own little deal, doing what young, single women do.

Linda met a nice man named Sam Williams. They dated for a while and then married. Sam had spent some time in Great Falls, Montana, when he was in the service. He liked it out there, and they agreed it would be a cool place to start their married life together. Their first daughter, Tara, was born while they were there. Within a year or so, they returned to Raleigh to be near family.

Sam got a job upon returning, and Linda stayed home with Tara and became a Tupperware sales representative. She did very well and hosted parties regularly. They had rented a small apartment but quickly ran out of room due to the large amounts of Tupperware items she needed to keep on hand. They found a larger home on the outskirts of Raleigh. Linda has always been business-savvy and did very well with the company. She won some nice trips because she did so well. Eventually, she ended up in a distributorship position and no longer hosted Tupperware parties.

After Sam and Linda's second daughter, Leah, was born on February 2, 1979, Linda retired from the Tupperware business. They moved to a nice country-style house not far from Mom and Dad's house. Sam got a good job at a huge research complex called Research Triangle Park, located between Raleigh, Chapel Hill, and Durham.

He worked a swing shift in the maintenance department, going back and forth from the day shift to the night shift. Someone had to be there at all hours to make sure the equipment was running correctly. When I would visit Linda during the day, sometimes Sam would be sleeping because he was working nights. They settled in and did this for a while.

In 1984, Linda began teaching a Bible-study class one night a week at the North Carolina Correctional Institution for Women in Raleigh. She was vetted thoroughly to work there and eventually became a fixture. She even offered her input at times to the powers that be as to whether or not she felt like an inmate would do well on the outside.

Many, if not most, of the women Linda counseled were in prison for murder. Many of them had killed their husbands or significant others because they were being abused physically, mentally, and sexually.

Linda began allowing some of the ladies—just one at a time—to live with her and her family for a while after they were paroled. They were of all races and ages. She took them right into her home. They, in turn, would help her around the house or help with the kids. Everybody recognized each woman as a member of the family. There was no, "Hey, be careful, she's a criminal." There couldn't have been a better environment for them—much better than a halfway house, I'm sure.

Linda's home was a tremendously loving environment for these ladies. No one was judged. Nobody talked about what the women did; they were on the same level as everybody else in the house. They ate meals with the family and were treated like everybody else. This must have had a big impact on them. Most of the ladies, after spending time in Linda's home, got jobs and lived full, loving, and successful lives. There's no question—it had to be because of Linda and her family.

Linda continued teaching the Bible study at the prison once a week for many years. As her daughters began to get older and didn't need as much supervision, she also began to get more involved with some other ministries. She was passionate about spreading the Gospel and helping people.

After Susan graduated from high school and turned eighteen, she began working. She met Wilson Scott, a shoe salesman at the same Boylan-Pearce department store where Mom had worked in the accounting department. Wilson had been married before and had a young daughter, Hunter. I think he had primary custody and his parents helped him out with her, but I'm not sure.

After dating for a couple of years, Susan and Wilson got married and moved into an apartment. They had a son, Jason, and then a daughter, Shannon. Even though Hunter was Susan's stepchild, Susan came into her life when she was around two years old and really fulfilled the mother role for her.

Unfortunately, Susan became addicted to prescription medication when she was young, and then alcohol, and could never shake it. I offered multiple times to get her into a rehabilitation facility, but she refused. Linda tried everything she could do to help Susan as well. Susan just had no interest in living a clean life. A little at a time, we watched her slip away from us. She was only fifty-three when she died in August 2006, two years after my dad had passed.

3

HAPPINESS: ANYTHING ON WHEELS

Growing up, I had a friend, Ronnie Green, who lived only a couple of blocks from North Hills Mall. I would spend the night at Ronnie's house maybe once a month, typically on a Friday night. Mom and Dad would give me a little spending money. After school, Ronnie and I would go to his house and then walk to the mall after dinner. I will always remember going to Hickory Farms to get a sample of that wonderful summer sausage.

Next door to the mall, there was a motorcycle shop. Ronnie and I would go in and look at the small, 90cc motorcycles. We both dreamed about getting one. I don't remember the exact price, but for us, it was a lot of money. I imagined myself riding that motorcycle on the trails behind my house, feeling the excitement of speed and the thrill of freedom—being able to go wherever I wanted. Soon, I got serious about this instead of just dreaming about it. I decided I was going to find some work and save enough money to buy one of those motorcycles.

Somehow, I got connected with a realtor who was selling homes for a developer who was building a new subdivision. His company hired me to mow the lawns of all the unsold houses. I was paid $5 per yard. Sometimes I'd get lucky—there would be three or four unsold houses next door to each other. I would mow them as if they were one big lawn and could knock them out quickly. I had this job for a couple of summers.

My dad loved the fact that I was working and earning my own money. He thought it was the greatest thing in the world. He made a point to drive me and our lawn mower to the place I needed to be in the morning. I would take my lunch and some water, and he would pick me up in the evening. Both Mom and Dad frequently drove station wagons, so there was always room to get that lawn mower in the back.

Now that I was making money, I was able to put the motorcycle on layaway. I was making regular payments on it and had it paid off before long. At age fifteen, I had my first set of wheels!

When I was growing up, the North Carolina Division of Motor Vehicles alternated the color of license plates from year to year. If last year's tags had red numbers on an off-white background and this year's tags had green numbers, it was easy for a police officer to see if you were driving with an expired tag.

I wasn't old enough to have my driver's license, so I couldn't get my own tag, but I found an old, expired one that I decided to use. The year 1970 was printed on the tag in green letters, and I needed it to be 1971 in red letters. I went to a hobby store and bought two small bottles of paint, the type you use to paint model cars. I got red paint for the numbers and off-white for the background. I matched the colors as well as I could to the current year's red and white tags and changed the 1970 to 1971.

My friends, Randy Bates and Walt Brandenburg, also had motorcycles. We liked to meet and go riding together. Sometimes, I would leave the house on a Friday and tell my parents that I was going to ride the trails to Randy's house and spend the night. I did intend to ride on the trails, but I also intended to ride on the streets with the doctored tag I had created. I'd take off through the backyard with some clothes and random items strapped on the back. When I got far enough away from the house that Mom and Dad couldn't hear the motorcycle anymore, I'd pull over, get the painted tag out from under the seat, and put it on the back. I had a helmet on, and my bike was street legal. I'd be careful to drive the speed limit while driving up and down the streets.

I felt like a fully bulletproof motorcycle rider.

Whenever it was time for me to go home the next day or when the weekend was over, I'd do the entire process in reverse. I'd head to the woods, stop to remove that tag, put it back under the seat, and drive home. I did a really good job of converting that 1970 tag to a 1971 and never got pulled over by the cops. My motorcycle became my escape until I got my first car.

A few months before I turned sixteen, my dad bought me my first car—a 1966 Plymouth Valiant. You talk about a no-game, dud car—but it was fine. I was tickled to death to have my own car. It was small and old, with a three-speed manual transmission on the column.

Mom, Dad, and I rode out to look at the car one day, and Dad bought it for $150. Mom drove her car back to the house. Dad and I got in that Valiant, and he drove it home. I couldn't believe it—I had a car! Dad took it to a repair shop there in town to get some dents out of it and have it painted. He paid for all of it. Dad had gotten cars for Linda and Susan when they were able to start driving also, but theirs were both a heck a lot nicer than that Valiant. Maybe they paid him back, while I didn't?

I didn't have my driver's license yet, but while the car was parked at the house, I could piddle with it, so it gave me something to do. When I finally turned sixteen, I had a car, and I was more than ready to drive. I got my license and drove the Valiant back and forth to school. I was thrilled I didn't have to ride the school bus anymore.

Two weeks later, I got in an accident. A man ran into the side of my car, and it was a total loss. After looking around a while, I found a really cool 1968 Camaro 327 four-speed. Again, I didn't have the money to buy it, so Dad bought it for me. Getting cars wasn't a problem—Dad was very generous about this. If I wanted a car, I went to Dad to plead my case, and he would get a car for me. I may have worked out a deal where I would pay him back or do some work for him. I can't really remember what the details were on this particular vehicle.

Buying cars, fixing them up, and having a lot of fun driving them brought me a lot of joy in life. It gave me something to look forward to while isolated out there on Lead Mine Road.

4

CHOOSING WORK OVER COLLEGE

I had very little interest in traditional classroom learning. I just didn't like it. The older I got, the more uncomfortable I felt in that environment. There was no expectation that I would go to college. In fact, Mom and Dad never even said the word "college" to me.

There was a program in my high school that would give you credit toward graduation if you had a job learning a trade. I signed up for that program, but I had yet to find a job. The guidance counselor at school called me one day and said I couldn't be in the program unless I got a job immediately. That afternoon, I told a friend of mine, Robbie Johnson, about it.

He said, "I've been working at Northside Auto Body as a helper, and I just quit to take another job. You could probably go over there and get a job."

I went down to Northside Auto Body, which was an auto paint and body-repair shop, and interviewed with the owner, Andy Barefoot. He gave me a job as a helper, which didn't really require any experience, but I would be learning a trade. It was a perfect fit for the school's requirement.

In this program, my class requirements were different than those for the students who planned to go to college. This was in my sophomore year, and under these guidelines, I had to take only three morning classes, and I worked in the afternoons. By my junior year, I had only two classes, and in my senior year, I had just one class—English. As the years passed, I spent more time working and less time at school. That was just fine with me.

As a "grunt worker," I sanded cars, taped them up to get them ready to paint, and swept the floor. It was not a glamorous job, but I appreciated it. I'd get there right after lunch every weekday, around 1:00 in the afternoon.

Andy was a nice guy. Ed Joyner was his right-hand guy and was there throughout my employment. Other paint and body technicians would come and go, but Ed and Andy always remained. Over time, they gradually gave me more responsibilities. Before I knew it, I was learning the paint and body-repair business, and Andy was giving me small pay increases.

I liked seeing the results of my work. When I'd finish a repair, I'd look at it and think, *This is pretty cool*. When I came across a difficult repair, I welcomed the challenge. I was determined to master whatever I was doing.

In my junior year, I could get to the body shop by 10:30 a.m. and then have a lunch break with Andy and Ed. When lunch time came, we decided if it was going to be Burger King or McDonald's. Ed and I would hop in one of our cars to go get the food. We'd come back, and the three of us would eat our lunch.

As time went on, I got better and better at repairing vehicles. I was good at it. I learned quickly, and I learned from a couple of good guys. I remember thinking, *This is probably going to be my career.*

By the time my senior year came around, having just that one English class, I was at the body shop most of each weekday. At some point, I just quit going to school. One day, I just got up in the morning and went to work instead of school.

Mom and Dad knew I had stopped going to school. They weren't overly upset about it because they knew I wasn't going to college, and they knew I had just one more class to finish before graduating. My thought was that I didn't have to have a diploma to get a job as a paint and body-repair guy. I don't think a lot of people at Millbrook High School knew I quit school, except for my closest friends. I just kind of slowly vanished.

Even though I was thriving in my job at Andy's repair shop, there were times when I thought that maybe I needed to look at some other options. I guess I wanted to make sure I was doing the right thing and not missing something. Even though I didn't have a formal education, I was a pretty smart guy. I felt like there might be something more for me out there somewhere—something other than beating on fenders of cars for the rest of my life.

When Linda was younger, she had worked at Wachovia Bank, a big bank in North Carolina that is now Wells Fargo. She worked in the check-processing department on the night shift. She enjoyed the work, so I thought I'd give a desk job a try.

I got a job at North Carolina National Bank, doing check processing on the night shift, just like Linda had at Wachovia. It was clerical work, but I didn't mind doing it. I worked from 6:00 p.m. to 2:00 a.m. I ran a proof machine, which was a huge adding machine, about the size of a piano, with about thirty rolls of tape. Each tape was for a different small community bank. North Carolina National was a big bank, and the staff processed its checks, as well as the checks for small community banks that didn't have check-processing departments of their own. When a batch of checks would come through from these banks, I'd click the appropriate roll of tape and enter the amount of each check.

After nine months or so, I decided those hours just didn't work for me. I asked Andy if I could go back to work at the body shop. He said yes, so I went back to work there, settled in, and decided this was what I was going to do indefinitely.

After work, I'd usually hit the road and go out for the evening. I got into a little trouble—not major stuff—but I got a lot of traffic tickets. Primarily because I wasn't paying attention.

As a result, I spent a lot of time at Carl Churchill's office. He was an attorney whose office was in downtown Raleigh, and his specialty was traffic violations. I got to know him on a first-name basis. I'd be at his office frequently, as I was usually just one ticket away from losing my driving privileges.

Carl Churchill and I would go to court, and he would get me out of all those tickets. I don't care what it was, the guy could get you out of it. He was smart, and he was recognized as a great attorney. Everyone knew Carl Churchill.

Remember how I said my dad was thrilled that I started my own lawn-mowing business and saved my own money to buy that 90cc motorcycle a few years earlier? Well, a lot of his pride in me eroded as I kept getting into trouble. I had gone from an enterprising young entrepreneur to a screw-up in his mind. I was on autopilot with no goals. I didn't give much consideration to where I wanted to wind up or what I wanted to do. I just went to work every day and worked on cars.

5

WHY ISN'T EVERYBODY IN DAYTONA BEACH?

Andy decided to close the shop for a week or ten days each summer so everyone could go on vacation at once. He thought this was a better strategy than for the three of us to go on vacations at different times.

My friends, Johnny and Steve, and I decided we would go to Daytona Beach one year. Johnny's parents were avid campers and had previously stayed at the Nova Family Campground there. We packed up the car and drove down to Florida. We arrived late at night and pitched our tent at the campground located just a few miles from Daytona Beach. We purchased a pass that allowed us to stay for six nights. The campground was going to be our home base.

The next morning, we left the campground to go to Daytona Beach. At the main road, we turned in the direction of a sign that said "Beaches." We didn't realize we were headed to New Smyrna Beach, about sixteen miles south of our destination. We didn't know we weren't in Daytona until the sign on the beach ramp said, "Welcome to New Smyrna Beach."

We were surprised to discover that we could drive on the beach. We had never driven on a beach, and it was a lot of fun. We drove north and went to Ponce Inlet, a big rock formation that crosses the beach and extends out into the ocean. We were sitting on the beach, enjoying the breeze, and listening to the waves. We had an idea. We decided that the next day, we would go back to Nova Campground, get our tent, and come pitch it on the beach at Ponce Inlet. We didn't realize it at the time, but camping wasn't allowed on the beach. We were typical naïve eighteen-year-olds.

During the daytime, there were a lot of people on the beach. New Smyrna was very popular because it was the closest beach to Orlando. We hung out there near our tent on the beach all day, and other people began coming out and pitching their tents as well. However, ours was a big eight-man tent with a floor, substantially larger than the other tents people were beginning to pitch. We were having a big time on the beach, wearing just shorts and no shirts. We didn't know anything about sunscreen, so we all got extremely sunburned. Because we had our six-day pass at the Nova Family Campground, we would drive back there in the evenings to take our showers.

The New Smyrna Beach Police Department had a Volkswagen dune buggy they used to patrol the beach late at night. A couple of nights, we could hear the patrolmen in the dune buggy just cutting up, having fun. They were driving over the dunes, spinning out sideways and flying high through the air. They never stopped to say anything to us about having the tent on the beach.

We camped there for the better part of a week. We spent our days at the inlet in New Smyrna Beach, and sometimes would go spend some time at Daytona Beach.

The day before we planned to leave, there were four or five tents on the beach, along with ours, like a "tent city." The police came by and said to us all, "Hey, folks, you can't camp here on the beach. You've got to pack your stuff and leave."

We were surprised they hadn't told us to leave before, but I was tickled to death that we had to leave. I'd never been so sunburned in my entire life. All three of us were just fried. The skin cancers that I'm having removed today are probably due to that trip. To make matters worse, sand would blow into our tent all day, so when we'd get in our sleeping bags at night, they would be full of sand. A sunburn and sand aren't a good combination.

We had a little money left, so we got a room at a small concrete-block motel called Beachside Motel. It took each of us about an hour to shower because of the pain. Johnny seemed to be tolerating the discomfort better than Steve and me.

Right next to the motel was Pappass Drive-In. In our room, there was a menu for Pappas. I told Johnny, "Get me the twenty-one-piece fried shrimp dinner." Johnny went over there and got us three to-go meals. When he returned with the food, I lay there in bed and ate the shrimp. It was just fantastic, and afterward, I was so full and content.

I remember getting between those clean sheets in that bed with the air conditioner turned on high. It was the closest thing I'd ever experienced to heaven on Earth. I turned out the light and went to sleep. It was probably the best night's sleep I've ever had.

The next morning, we loaded up the car and drove home.

That trip to Daytona Beach and New Smyrna Beach always stuck in the back of my mind. I often thought, *Why isn't everybody in Daytona Beach?* We'd had such a great time. I had loved the weather, the fun beaches, the smell of the coast, and the coastal breeze.

The more I thought about the trip, the more I wanted to actually live there. I knew it would take a lot of planning and I'd have to save some money before moving, but I could make it happen. I would pay off my car, have my car insurance paid for one year in advance, and save enough money to get me by until I was able to get a job, and *then* I would make the move.

By now, most of my high-school friends had either moved away or were renting their own apartments or houses in town. A few of them rented small houses together out in the country somewhere. I was still living at Mom and Dad's and saving my money. I had the entire upstairs to myself. Sometimes I'd have the entire house to myself. They had bought a small vacation house down at Atlantic Beach, so a lot of weekends, they'd take off and drive down there. It was a pretty good deal.

When I would go out with a few of the guys, we would sometimes have a little too much fun. I'm sure I initiated it at times. One weekend, Mike Walsher and I left a local bar called Charlie Goodnight's in my car. Some girl said, "Hey, follow us." We followed her and her friends to the city of Cary. Today, Cary and Raleigh have grown together, but back then, you had to drive on a two-lane road for about ten minutes to get to Cary from Raleigh.

The girl driving the car was driving slowly so we could keep up with them. We'd stop at a stop sign every now and then and talk through the car windows. At some point, she pulled into an upscale neighborhood and started driving faster, so I started driving faster. Maybe they were late getting home; I have no idea. She pulled into a garage, so I stopped out in front of the house to wait for her to come tell us the plan. A couple of minutes later, the girl's dad opened the front door and stormed out carrying a shotgun. Now, this wasn't a rural country bumpkin out in the boonies. This guy had an upscale home in an upscale neighborhood in Cary, and he was running toward me with a shotgun!

I quickly realized we had to get out of there, and fast, but the house was on a cul-de-sac. We were at a dead end with no easy exit. I hurriedly turned the car around so we could leave. The dad got into his Lincoln Continental with a guy who looked to be the girl's older brother, and as we were passing back by their house, they came flying up behind us. I said, "Oh my gosh, we've got this guy with a gun chasing us." Because I had never been to the neighborhood before, I didn't know which way to go and soon became boxed in on a dead-end road. The guy parked his vehicle in the middle of the street, blocking it. Little did we know he had called the police before leaving his house, telling them some guys were chasing his daughter and to get out there.

To get away from the girl's dad, I didn't have a choice but to drive right past him. When I did, he jumped out of his car and shot out my left rear tire with the shotgun. I started losing control of the vehicle, but I didn't slow down. I couldn't. I was scared to death and took off even faster down the road. A car was approaching with blue lights. It was a sheriff's deputy responding to the call the dad had made. I knew better than to try to outrun him, especially with a flat tire, so I stopped my car.

The police officer said, "Let me see your driver's license. What are y'all doing?" I told him the story and that we were just going to head back home when this guy shot out my tire. He said, "Get out of the car."

I quickly let him know that I was not getting out of the car until he got the shotgun away from the guy. "I can't believe you all haven't disarmed him. He just shot my tire. The guy could have killed us," I said.

Finally, they took his gun away, and the man left. I realized that Mike was no longer there. I didn't know where he went or how he had left, but he was long gone. The officer took me to the Cary Police Department to administer a breathalyzer test. Not surprisingly, I was intoxicated.

The officer then took me to the Wake County Jail in Raleigh. I was processed and put in a cell.

I didn't want to call Linda. I was afraid the first thing she would do was call Mom and Dad. I felt like my chances were better with Susan and Wilson. Somehow, Wilson got me out on his recognizance early the next morning without having to post my bond. I don't know how he did it because he and Susan didn't qualify. They lived in an apartment and had no assets. I suspect it was because he told them I was Ernest Hill's son. My dad knew the Wake County sheriff and some local judges as well, and he was well respected throughout the community.

My car, with the left rear tire shot out, was impounded. I hired Carl Churchill to get me out of the DUI charge. I set up a meeting with him for the next Monday evening. Churchill met with all his clients in the evening because he was in court every day, all day long, defending people.

On Monday morning, my mom was reading the newspaper.

She said, "My God. Carl Churchill died."

I said, "What?!"

He had suffered a heart attack and died on Friday. This was unfortunate in general, and more specifically for me, because now he couldn't defend me. I knew his secretary well because I was one of his "better" clients, so I called her and expressed my condolences. I was hoping for a referral to another attorney, and she gave me one, thankfully. I hired him to represent me.

The result was that I lost my driving privileges for one year, but I did receive a "work permit" allowing me to drive to work. The work permit was simply a piece of paper from the courts stating I could drive only from 6:00 a.m. to 11:00 p.m. and only for trips related to work. I couldn't drive to see friends, go out to eat, etc. Trust me, I adhered to this policy. I wasn't going to take any chances.

My parents were not happy, naturally, that I'd gotten myself into this debacle. I think, at the time, it just reinforced my dad's belief that I wasn't going to amount to anything. Just another Larry screw-up.

At some point, Andy decided to close the shop on Fridays. We would work four days a week, ten hours per day, Monday through Thursday. I'm still trying to figure out who in the business world shuts down on Fridays. A lot of customers came in on Fridays to get estimates on their cars. I didn't think it was a good move for the business—but it was for me.

Somebody told me about a guy who owned a repair garage in Lizard Lick, a small town about twenty miles east of Raleigh. The small town had one crossroad with a flashing light. There was a little post office on one corner and a repair shop on the other. People in that area didn't want to drive all the way to Raleigh to get their cars repaired. The owner did mechanical repairs from 7:00 a.m. to 5:00 p.m. every day. The garage was empty after hours, and another guy would go in at night and on weekends to do minor body repairs for the local people, but he had recently left.

I drove to Lizard Lick, found the garage owner, and asked him if I could use his garage in the evenings. He agreed and then showed me which section of the garage I was to use. He said he would have vehicles there for me to work on.

This guy didn't seem knowledgeable about pricing, or maybe he just wasn't comfortable with it, so I handled this piece as well. I would look at the cars, assess the damage, and give people estimates. After finishing the needed repairs, I would give the garage owner 10 to 15 percent of the repair.

Apparently, he felt like it was a good deal for him. It was definitely a good deal for me.

At that time, I lived about twenty minutes from my day job at Andy's body shop. At the end of the workday, I'd leave his shop around 6:00 and drive in the opposite direction of home for an additional twenty minutes to Lizard Lick. On the way there, I would stop at Burger King to get dinner, which usually consisted of a burger, fries, and a Coke. I'd get to Lizard Lick at about 6:30. It was a quiet place, and I could get a lot done by myself in the evenings. I'd work on the cars for about three hours, until 9:30 or 10:00 at night. Then I'd make the forty-minute drive back to my parents' house because of the 11:00 driving-permit curfew. I'd get up the next morning and do it again.

On Fridays, Saturdays, and Sundays, I drove to Lizard Lick and spent the whole day there. Work was my entire life.

During this time, I was making decent money during the day at Northside Auto Body because I was an experienced auto body-repair guy, but I was making more money at Lizard Lick. I was working there evenings and three full days a week.

I was serious about not getting into any more trouble. If Johnny, Steve, or Danny wanted to pick me up, I might occasionally go out one evening, but there wasn't a whole lot of this. I focused on working and saving money.

The twelve-month period went by pretty quickly. Although I had saved some money, I didn't feel like I'd saved quite enough to make my move to Florida without being under financial pressure. Now my driving privileges had been reinstated, but I felt I needed to continue doing the same routine, working at both places, for several more months.

Toward the end of that year, I decided to head down to Daytona Beach for a few days in my 1969 Firebird. I had paid my auto insurance for a year in advance, and I had paid off all my other bills. I wanted to check it out, spend a little time there, and see if that's really where I wanted to live. I knew that sometimes I hadn't made the wisest decisions in the past, so I was being overly cautious before moving.

When I arrived in Daytona Beach, I rented an efficiency room and spent some time getting to know the area—going to the beach, meeting people, and having a good time. I've never had a difficult time doing things by myself. I've never minded it. It probably has something to do with all that time I spent out there on Lead Mine Road by myself. I have always enjoyed doing things alone.

Daytona Beach felt right. I knew I could consider dropping anchor there for a bit, so I started looking for a job. There were several paint and body shops in the area. Some were independent, and some were in dealerships. I knew there wouldn't be a big surplus of qualified paint and body technicians down there because it's not an industry a lot of people wanted to get into back then. (Nowadays, no one wants to get into it. That's the reason most new-car dealers no longer have paint and body shops).

I wasn't getting anywhere on the job search. One day, I was talking with a guy who owned one of the independent shops. I told him what I was looking for and said I had gone to several shops but wasn't having any luck.

"You're having no luck because you haven't even moved here yet," he said. "Look, you're a young guy. Everybody your age wants to move to Daytona Beach. They go, 'Oh my God, Daytona!' and they want to move down here. They come here for three or four months. They get lonely. They miss their families. They realize how hot and humid it is. They get their bellies full of the beach and girls and drinking, and then they go back home."

Then he said, "If you're still here in ninety days, come back and see me. I'm not telling you that I'll hire you then, but the chances are a lot better after you've lived here for a while."

That made sense, but it turned out that I didn't have to do this after all.

I remembered that when Steve, Johnny, and I had gone to New Smyrna Beach, we had passed a small Chevrolet dealership on US 1. The efficiency I was renting for the week in Daytona Beach was also on US 1, about twenty miles away from New Smyrna Beach. When I was ready to leave, I had a choice to make. I could either take a left and head back to Raleigh, or I could make a right and go to New Smyrna Beach to check out the Chevy store. I don't know what prompted me to make the decision, but I turned right.

The dealership had changed ownership since my trip with the guys a couple years earlier. The store was now named Higginbotham Chevrolet Oldsmobile. The new owner was Dennis Higginbotham.

I drove around back to the paint and body shop. It was old, beaten up, and rough. The body shop I had worked at in Raleigh was one of the very few air-conditioned paint and body shops I'd ever seen in my life. Andy went all out. In the mornings, we would get our cars situated in there, he would pull the doors down, and we could work in our short sleeves year-round. We didn't have to wear a coat; it was comfortable all the time. Also, all the equipment was state-of-the-art.

The floors in this shop at Higginbotham weren't even concrete. They were asphalt. Somebody had just built the shop on top of asphalt. Next to a door where a sign read "Office" stood a good-looking guy who was well-groomed and dressed nicely in management-type clothing. I introduced myself, told him I was looking for a job, and we talked for a little bit. His name was Ted Powers, and he was the manager of the body shop.

Ted said the previous owner didn't do much to attract business. It was just a little old sleepy dealership when Dennis Higginbotham bought it. He said he, Dennis, and the other managers were trying to get it going. We discussed my experience and background.

"You know what? I've got two guys here, and I need two and a half," Ted said. "I almost need three. As a matter of fact, the owner and I have already discussed it some, but you're going to need to talk to him. He bought the dealership less than a year ago, and he interviews every potential employee."

The dealership had fewer than twenty employees, so I understood why Dennis would want to interview everyone. He had invested everything in the dealership and wanted to get the right team in place. In the average dealership today, if a manager hires somebody in the service or parts department or in the paint and body shop, that person might not meet the owner of that dealership for a month, six months, a year—or maybe ever.

Ted took me to the Sales Department to introduce me to Dennis. He asked me where I was originally from, and we chatted for a short while. Then we got down to business and talked about what he was looking for in his new dealership. While we were sitting there, he picked up the phone and called Andy Barefoot back in Raleigh. Dennis introduced himself and said he was interviewing me.

Apparently, Andy gave me a good reference because Dennis hung up the phone and said, "Andy speaks very highly of you." He paused and then added, "OK, we'll give it a shot."

He hired me on the spot. I agreed to be there, ready to work, in two weeks.

6

MY MOVE TO FLORIDA

I turned twenty-one years old in 1977 and was headed to Daytona Beach to begin the next phase of my life. A guy I knew, Tim Latta, wanted to go with me. Tim was a mountain guy, not a beach guy. He had really fair skin, glasses, and curly, frizzy hair. I don't think I ever saw him wear a pair of shorts. Tim worked as a cabinet maker. He had been doing it for a long time and was really good at it. I wondered why he wanted to go to Daytona Beach but didn't question him.

About five o'clock one morning, I drove my Firebird out of the driveway. I had a U-Haul trailer hitched to it with all my tools and a few other belongings. Mom and Dad were standing on the front porch, waving. Mom was crying. Mom had always been a big worrier, a fearful person, and I think she suffered somewhat from depression. (Dad may have been crying also, but his would have been tears of joy.) I was sad to leave them, but I could hardly wait to start my new life in Florida.

Tim was going to follow me there in his Ford van, so we met at a predetermined location and then traveled straight to Daytona Beach. Upon arriving, we stayed in a small motel room for a couple of days so we could get our bearings. We found a two-bedroom, one-bath apartment in South Daytona to rent. Tim found a job within two days.

We were officially living in Florida now, rocking and rolling.

Tim and I didn't have much in common, but we got along fine. He would go to a bar and have a drink every now and then, but he didn't like going to the beach. He was one of those guys who wanted everyone to go back to the house, sit around, drink beer, and watch a ball game. Although we lived in the same apartment, we essentially lived totally separate lives.

In the paint and body business, you're compensated a percentage of the labor charge for the repair. It's not a salaried job. For example, if the labor on a repair job is $100, you might get paid 40 percent of that amount, which would be $40. When you finish one job, you start on the next. You're mostly in control of how much you make, depending on your speed. If you do good work efficiently, you can make good money.

When I got there, the body shop didn't have much business. Some of the cars needed something as minor as a touch-up to a blemish in the paint. Other cars needed more extensive work after being in accidents. I preferred to work on the cars that had been hit harder because I could give that specific job all my attention without bouncing around, fixing a little something on this car and a little something on others, for peanuts. With jobs that involved a good amount of labor, I had more control over my pay because if I could fix that car quickly and efficiently, I would make more money.

When a big job came in, it would be assigned to a repair tech who was available at that time. If you were finishing up a job from the previous day, the manager wanted you to finish that job, obviously, before starting on a new one. When five o'clock rolled around, I would stay late and finish the job I was working on at the time. I wanted to be the guy who didn't have anything to do the next morning so I could get my hands on the good jobs. Plus, because the shop wasn't very busy, there wasn't always enough work for the three of us. If you missed a good job, you never knew when you would get another.

Because I worked late many weeknights, I would go straight home after work. During the week, I was all business. Now, the weekends were a different story. But boy, when the clock struck 5:00 each afternoon, the other two paint and body techs, Pat and Bob, dropped what they were doing and bolted out the door. Pat was eager to get home because his girlfriend was a server at a restaurant. She got off at the same time he did, and they would sit on their front porch and smoke marijuana. As for Bob, he had a small mechanical shop on his property, and he always had other jobs going on out there. Both of them did their eight and hit the gate.

Pretty much right away, Dennis Higginbotham noticed that I often worked late. He was in his mid-thirties, which was young for a dealership owner. In the evenings before going home, he would walk around to see what was going on at the dealership. He was a smart guy. He kept his eyes on everything and saw every single employee every day. When I was working in the evening, I would see him on the other side of the window, with his hands cupped against the glass, watching me. One day, Dennis asked me why I worked late, and I told him it was because I could finish up what I was doing and be ready for the good jobs the next morning.

He said, "You know what, Larry? That makes a lot of sense. Very smart."

This is how I originally got on his radar. He liked my work ethic. The other techs and the manager knew what I was doing, too. When Friday rolled around, I typically got the biggest paycheck.

One afternoon, I was standing at the front of the body shop, talking to Ted, the manager. Dennis pulled up in the company car he was driving, a black Corvette. Corvettes were made of fiberglass, and Dennis's had a nasty gash in the passenger side door. He was pretty hot. He bounced out of the car and said, "Damn it! I was at the barber shop. As I was leaving, a guy backed into my car." He offered Ted the keys and said he needed to get it repaired.

Ted told Dennis he didn't have any techs who could repair fiberglass. They didn't know yet that I was very knowledgeable and experienced at this. First of all, we had done a lot of work on Corvettes at Andy's shop. Secondly, we did all the repairs and warranty work for two boat manufacturers. Generally, there were always a couple of fiberglass boats in Andy's shop.

I said, "I can fix it."

Ted said, "Really?"

"Yes, it's not a problem."

Dennis said, "Great" and tossed me the keys. I pulled the car into the shop and started working on it. Repairing fiberglass is totally different than repairing metal. It requires a lot of cutting with a hacksaw blade to cut out the bad parts, and you have to remove all the splintered fiberglass edges and lay out fiberglass matting. You then mix resin and hardener with the matting, cover the damaged area, and put heat lamps on it to speed up the drying time. Sometimes it takes three or four hours, and sometimes overnight, for the matting to dry.

The other two technicians couldn't believe I could repair Corvettes. They were fascinated. It was almost like I was performing surgery, and they were med students watching over my shoulder. When I finished, Dennis and Ted were impressed that the passenger door looked as good as new.

One day, Dennis walked into the body shop with a friend, a well-dressed guy. Dennis pointed to me and said, "Here's the guy who's going to fix your car." Right then, a wrecker pulled up towing an orange Corvette that'd had the crap knocked out of the entire front end. It was an insurance repair. An insurance adjuster came out, looked at the damage, and wrote an estimate. It took me about three weeks to complete the repairs. The repair work came out great, looking like new.

We didn't have a helper in the body shop at the time to clean vehicles after we had repaired them. Realizing this was a good friend of Dennis's, I wanted to make sure it was not only repaired, but meticulously cleaned inside and out when the owner came to get it. I took the car down to the wash area myself and cleaned it. I wanted Dennis to be proud.

The decision I made to invest the additional time to clean the car paid off when Dennis and his friend saw it. Now I wasn't only *on* Dennis's radar—I *stayed* on his radar.

Steve Burton, one of the three guys who had gone on our first trip to Daytona and New Smyrna Beach, was living in Raleigh. He and his long-time girlfriend, Renee, were getting married. My roommate, Tim, and I were driving back to North Carolina for the wedding. By this time, Tim had decided he'd had his fill of Florida and wanted to move back home. It wasn't a surprise.

Tim and I drove back to Raleigh in his van on a Friday evening after work. We drove through the night. He dropped me off at Mom and Dad's house around 4:00 a.m. and said, "I'll see you at the wedding." After getting a few hours of sleep, I visited with my parents and then went to the wedding that afternoon. Tim wasn't there—and I haven't seen Tim Latta since he dropped me off that morning.

I had taken Monday off work, so I booked a one-way flight from Raleigh to Daytona on Eastern Airlines. I was twenty-one years old, and it was the first time I had ever flown. I think the ticket was $60. Mom drove me to the airport and dropped me off, probably crying again.

When I got back to Florida, I told the landlord whom Tim and I had been renting from that he had moved back to North Carolina. I had to pay a small penalty, but they let me out of the lease. I relocated to 107 Due East Street in

New Smyrna Beach. It was a small, furnished one-bedroom duplex I rented from a nice lady named Nancy Conklin. I lived there for the next few years.

7

HILL'S PAINT AND BODY SHOP

I really enjoyed working at the dealership, but there wasn't enough work for three of us. I knew I could make more money at a place that was busier. One day, someone told me about a guy named Ray Rhinehart, who owned a salvage yard in town. He also owned a small paint and body shop that had closed. Ray didn't own the property. He rented it from an attorney in town for $300 a month, but he owned the equipment inside the shop.

When I went to the salvage yard, I found Ray and talked to him. He was a mover and shaker. Don't for a minute think that just because the guy is wearing some old work clothes and he's not well-kempt and his hair is going all over the place and his shirt's torn that he's in bad shape financially.

There are a lot of ways to make money in the salvage-yard business. I've known salvage-yard owners all my life, a couple of them well. Some of them have shared the details of how the business works. These guys can do very well.

Ray told me where he lived and said to pick him up at 6:30 that evening. It wasn't far from the dealership and was a much nicer home than what I expected after having seen the junkyard.

When I picked him up, he looked like a totally different person. He was well dressed and groomed. He said he wanted to shoot pool at a little dive bar about a half a mile from his house. When we went inside, Ray racked up the balls and ordered a pitcher of beer. We shot pool and drank beer until around midnight. Throughout the evening, he'd tell me a little about his history and ask me about mine. He shared with me some details about his business.

Salvage-yard owners are required to have an auto dealer's license. Even though they are buying old, wrecked cars, there has to be a paper trail of the sales. Therefore, Ray had a dealer's license. He would buy old junk cars that ran pretty well but needed body repairs. He would repair, paint, and sell them. He knew how to make money every way possible. I think this was his original purpose for having the body shop, but for some reason, it never materialized.

Ray said the equipment was valued at $3,000. I could purchase it for this amount and then assume the $300 lease payment he was paying to a local attorney who owned the property.

I told him I didn't have any money, which I'm sure he already knew.

"Here's what I'll do," he said. "The shop's been closed for a while. You're not going to open the doors and suddenly have a flood of customers arriving. I will rent you the equipment, and you pay the $300 monthly lease payment to the property owner. I'll give you some cars to fix while you're getting started so you'll be able to make these payments."

The following day after work, I drove over to take a look around the shop. Even though I wasn't a business guy at that time—not at all—I was confident I could make this work.

I resigned from the dealership without speaking to Dennis. I just told Ted, the manager, and he understood. I said, "Half the time, I'm sitting around here doing nothing. I'm going to go over there and see if I can make this thing work at Ray Rhinehart's."

For the next two days, I did nothing but clean my new shop and all the equipment, figuring out what equipment worked and what didn't. I needed some supplies—Bondo, sandpaper, paint thinner, primer, etc.—but I didn't have money to buy them.

When I had worked at the Chevy Olds dealership, we bought our materials and supplies from a paint-supply store in town. If I needed paint, I would call the supplier and order it.

I had somewhat of a relationship with the paint-supply owner. One day, I sat down with him and told him I needed some supplies to get started. I said, "I'm going to rent Ray Rhinehart's shop. I need you to give me a credit account because I don't have the money to pay for the supplies." I needed about $100 worth of materials (which would probably cost $500 today).

He agreed to do this. He told me he would bill me at the end of the month and that I couldn't charge anything else until I paid him for these supplies. As time went on, I had a full charge account with him. I was able to open my shop, but I didn't have any business right away because it was off the beaten path, on a two-lane rural road. My thought was, *Build it, and they will come.*

Ray knew I didn't have much business, so he would occasionally bring me an old, wrecked car to repair. I'd say, "Ray, my God. Do you have a fender for this thing at your junkyard?"

He would reply, "It doesn't need a fender. Just beat the dent out and put a little Bondo on it." That was Ray's canned reply: "Just put a little Bondo on it."

He was quite a salesman. When I would say, "Ray, it'll take forever to repair that fender," he would say, "Ah, you can do it. You're good."

Ray continued to bring me those hunks of junk, and he would tell me how much he was going to pay for the repairs. I didn't give him a price; he would tell me, and it was usually about 50 percent of the price that I would have quoted. In addition to paying me a rock-bottom price for the repairs, he would also take a portion of that amount to offset my renting his equipment.

You talk about barely keeping your head above water. I was barely making it, but I kept at it, day in and day out.

Winners never quit, and quitters never win.

During those early years, I'd stop by Hathaway's Food Store to buy my two "go-to" foods: a pack of eight hot dogs and four boxes of Kraft macaroni with the powdered cheese.

Four boxes cost a dollar. I had one of those little electric hot-dogger gadgets where you stick the end of a hot dog on each metal probe and then close the cover to cook them. I'm going to tell you—four hot dogs and one box of macaroni and cheese will fill a guy up just fine.

The small, furnished duplex I lived in was next to the Intracoastal Waterway. At the end of our street was a little pier that extended out into the water. It was a public pier, but the only people who ever used it were the ones who lived on the dead-end piece of that road where I lived. Actually, I don't ever recall walking down to that pier and anyone else being there. It was almost like my private little pier.

Once in a while, I would take a break from the hot dogs and macaroni, and I'd catch some fish for dinner. I had a fishing pole, and I kept shrimp in the freezer for bait. I'd take a couple out, thaw them under water in the sink, and go to the pier with my fishing pole. Within a few minutes, I would catch two or three whiting that were about half a pound apiece. I had watched my mom clean and cook fish for many years, so I knew how to do it. I'd clean the fish and fry them whole.

Whether it was the hot dogs and mac and cheese or the fried fish, I went to bed every night with a full belly. For the most part, life was good.

There I was, all by myself, trying to make things work. I was constantly worried about my finances. You know the rest of the story from my introduction to this book. I was continuing to practice positive thinking and even turned Dr. Peale's book, *The Power of Positive Thinking*, into a personal workbook. I'd highlight and underline passages so that if I was struggling in a particular area, I could refer to them quickly.

I continued trying to make things work and continued to worry about my finances. So I would read Dr. Peale's book, and it seemed like every passage in it was written for me. Here's just one example of a passage that hit me hard:

"Formulate and stamp indelibly on your mind a mental picture of yourself as succeeding. Hold this picture tenaciously. Never permit it to fade. Your mind will seek to develop the picture... Do not build up obstacles in your imagination."

—Norman Vincent Peale

For my entire life, I always had a black and white view of the progress I was making. I felt I was either succeeding or failing. I have since come to learn that just because you don't succeed at something doesn't mean you failed. It means you have learned.

I've also learned that we only have so much energy to put into something each day. When you put half your energy into worrying about failing, you have only half your energy left to use toward succeeding.

Don't waste any energy on things that are out of your control.

Dr. Peale's advice is powerful on its own, but what gives it an unparalleled level of comfort and wisdom for me is that he bases all his advice and guidance on the Bible. During the times when I struggled, it sometimes felt things would never turn around for me. Knowing God was with me and guiding me gave me the strength I needed to turn my negative thoughts into positive ones.

I also learned that life is full of victories and disappointments. The only emotion that is stronger than fear is faith. If you have fear inside you, you need to reach in there, pull that fear out, and replace it with a big dose of faith. That's one of the major points of Dr. Peale's book.

Now, I'm not going to tell you that I conquered my fear after reading the book one time. I have regressed many times. The difference is that since that day when I felt my fear lift in the shop, I know what I need to do now when I start feeling fearful. I consciously replace my negative thoughts with positive thoughts. It keeps me from wallowing in worry, and it reminds me to trust God with all things.

8

SELLING MY CAR TO PAY THE RENT

Nancy Conklin, the woman I rented the duplex from, lived with her husband and their six or seven kids on the corner, right next to the duplex. One day, she showed up at my shop and said, "Larry, your rent check bounced."

I'd never bounced a check in my life. I didn't monitor my account very closely, and I paid most of my bills in cash. The only time I wrote a check was when I paid my rent. I was devastated and embarrassed. I said, "Nancy, I'm sorry. Give me two days, and I'll have it handled."

She said, "Not a problem, Larry. I know you will."

That was a Wednesday morning. Every Wednesday night in Daytona Beach on Highway 92, there was a public auto auction. The public could sell their own cars. There was a group of sharp, savvy car dealers who would be there.

They knew if someone was selling their car at this auction, they needed some money quickly. An auction/wholesaler isn't the best place to get the most money for your car. If you're selling your car at an auction, you're basically Larry Hill, a guy who needs some money right now.

I drove my car to the auction that night and took the title. My '69 Firebird looked almost new. Every car I had ever owned in my life was nice. I always had the nicest cars because it was important to me. I was thinking the car was going to sell for around $1,600. This was in 1977, and $1,600 was a lot of money. I knew the car was worth more than what I was going to get for it. I could not have begun to imagine that my car would bring only $825. It was a huge disappointment to me. It was the nicest car there. Buyers didn't go there expecting to spend a thousand, $1,200, or $1,300; they were buying $200 and $300 cars. The car dealer who bought my Firebird was a sharp guy. He was the high bidder at $825 and may have been the only bidder.

I was now forty miles from home, with no transportation, and it was around eleven o'clock at night. Down the highway I walked, heading home, hoping to catch a ride. Finally, someone picked me up and took me about halfway before he had to go in a different direction. When he dropped me off, I continued walking. Around midnight, an older guy picked me up. He was headed past New Smyrna down to Oak Hill. I thought he was going to drop me off on the main road closest to my house, since he was headed farther down the road. I'd then have about an hour's walk home. The guy was very nice, and I guess he felt bad for me. He said, "Hey, I've got time." He took me all the way to my duplex.

When I got up the next morning, I pulled out my little Yamaha 125 Enduro motorcycle that I had bought shortly after I moved to Florida. Since the days of my 90cc motorcycle back in Raleigh, I'd always had a passion for off-road motorcycle riding. Although my 125 was street-legal, it wasn't suitable for daily transportation; however, it was all I had now. I drove it to my local bank and explained to the teller that I needed to cash the check I'd gotten from the auction.

The lady said, "Oh you can't cash that check here. It's written on an out-of-town bank. You can deposit it and wait for it to clear, but that would probably take five days."

I told her I couldn't wait five days.

She said, pointing to the name on the check, "Well, then, you have to take it to this bank."

I drove straight from my bank to the Chevy dealership, where a friend of mine worked. He had a Honda 350, a much better street bike. When I got to the dealership, I asked him two things—first, "Can I borrow your motorcycle? I can't drive mine to Sanford" and second, "Where is Sanford?"

He gave me the directions, and I took off on his Honda 350 and drove to the bank in Sanford. I cashed the check and had $825 in my pocket. I drove straight back to Nancy Conklin's house and paid her the $155 I owed her. Less than twenty-four hours after she had gone to my shop and said my rent check bounced, I paid her.

I said, "Nancy, I apologize. It will never happen again."

Then I drove my friend's 350 back to the Chevy dealership, got on my little 125, and drove to my shop to start working.

That was a humbling experience, and it could've crushed me if I had let it get to me. But there wasn't a lot of time for me to feel sorry for myself. Selling my car to pay the rent was just what I had to do.

From my parents, I had learned you do what you're supposed to do. If you give someone your word, you fulfill that commitment. And guess what? You don't write somebody a bad check for your rent. It's worthless to them. If you do something wrong, the first thing you'd better do is make it right.

While I was working on Rhinehart's junky cars, trying to stay afloat, an older doctor brought his truck to the shop. Someone had referred him to me. The truck wasn't beat up, but it had a lot of minor damage.

He said, "Larry, this truck runs well, and it's a great truck for my farm. I'd like to get the exterior damage fixed, and I want the truck painted. I'm in no hurry. I just use the truck on my farm. If it takes two weeks, three weeks, a month, I don't care. Just do a good job."

I gave him a price, and he said it was fine. He was a nice guy.

With my Firebird gone, I was still using the little Yamaha 125 for transportation, but I couldn't carry groceries home on it or take my laundry to the laundromat. At that time, I was taking my laundry to the laundromat in a basket and dropping it off. The ladies there would wash, dry, and fold it for me.

Now, this old doctor's truck had some primer and Bondo spots on it, but it was drivable. I'd stay at the shop working on the body repairs until dark, probably nine o'clock. Then I'd drive the old doctor's truck down to Pappass restaurant. I'd park the truck around back because I never knew if I'd run into the guy. I'd order some food to go and then drive the truck home, eat my meal, and go to bed. I would get up about five o'clock the next morning, in the pitch black, and drive the truck back to Pappass for breakfast. I would get an egg and cheese sandwich and a cup of coffee and take it back to my shop, arriving before sunlight. For a week, I worked from before sunlight until after dark to make sure I wasn't seen driving the doctor's truck.

I needed to get some wheels of my own, so the next Wednesday evening, I went back to that same auction where I'd sold my Firebird. I bought a gold-colored Buick Skylark four-door sedan. I don't remember what year it was, but I paid $350 for it and man, it was ugly. At least now I had a car.

I drove it home, and right when I pulled into the driveway, I saw a little light flashing on the dash. It was the "Engine hot" light. When I got out, I could tell the car was running hot, but I was too exhausted to worry about it then. The next morning, I removed the radiator cap and saw there was no water in it. I filled it with water and limped the car back to my body shop, which was a fifteen-minute drive. Once I got to the shop and could look at it more closely, I saw that the radiator was busted, and someone had tried to repair it. I grabbed one of Rhinehart's old cars from the shop and drove down to his salvage yard, about a mile away. I said, "Hey, I need a radiator." Ray said he had a car out back that might have a radiator that would match mine.

I walked back there and made my way through the thick, high, snake-infested grass to the car. I slid under the car, just waiting any moment for a big water moccasin or something to bite me. I removed the radiator and took it to my shop. It was a fit. Yes! Now I had my own transportation again.

One Friday night a few weeks later, I wanted to get out and do something. I'd been working from sunup to sundown every day. I drove over to ABC, a bar in town.

Of course, in a small town, when you go out you're always going to see someone you know. I got a beer and spotted Scott Bowser, a guy who had worked in the Parts Department at the Chevy store when I worked there. I sat down next to him, and we talked for a while. Scott then looked around and said, "Hey, nothing's going on here. Let's go over to Breakers to see if anything's happening there."

ABC is on the mainland, and Breakers is on the beach. To get to Breakers, you have to go over the North Causeway, which is a big bridge that takes you over the Intracoastal Waterway to Flagler Avenue. Flagler is probably six blocks long, and Breakers is at the end of it, directly on the beach.

Scott rode with me there. We saw some other friends and had a couple of beers, catching up with everyone. After a while, we decided it was time to head back. I had to work the next morning. When we got in my car to leave, it wouldn't move forward. I put it in reverse to back out of the parking spot, and reverse worked fine. However, when the car was in drive, it wouldn't move. It reacted as if it was in neutral. I messed with the shifter and nothing happened. By then, it was around midnight, and Scott said, "What are we going to do?"

I said, "I guess I'm going to have to drive to ABC in reverse."

"You're going to *back* this car all the way to ABC?"

"I have no choice," I said.

I backed the car onto Flagler Avenue. I was driving in the same direction as other cars; I was just going backward. If you've ever tried to drive a car in reverse with any amount of speed, you know the car can get away from you in a minute—you can easily lose control. I was going slower than the other traffic, so I was sure I was causing a backup. Some drivers were going around me, beeping their horns, and some were flipping me off, but I had to do what I had to do. I began to get a little nervous as I approached the Causeway Bridge, but I backed the car over the bridge down the causeway to Riverside Drive. I took a couple of side roads and made my way to Lytle Avenue, a four-lane road. Fortunately, when I got to Lytle Avenue, the light was green.

There we were, backing across Lytle Avenue. Thank God we were almost to ABC. Well, guess who was sitting at the traffic light? A New Smyrna Beach police officer. He turned on his lights, spun his vehicle around, and pulled me over. Because I was driving backward, the officer was facing the front of my car. I backed off to the side of the road and stopped. He walked up and said, "Let me see your driver's license. What are you doing?"

Handing him my license, I said, "Officer, I'm just two blocks from where I need to be. My buddy's car is at ABC. We just need to get it."

Knowing the officer was still wondering why I was driving in reverse, I explained to him, "The transmission stopped working while we were at Breakers."

I probably didn't need to tell a cop at midnight that I was headed to one bar from another bar while in reverse, but I continued my story. He put his hands up and made a time-out signal, as a coach does in a football game.

"Time out. Are you telling me you backed this car all the way here from Breakers?" the officer asked.

"Yes, sir. And in two blocks, I'm home free."

He handed my driver's license back to me, thought for a moment, and then said, "I've seen nothing." He got in his patrol car and left.

I backed the car into the ABC parking lot and left it there. Scott dropped me off at my house and headed home.

I emerged unscathed from a situation that could have ended badly, but I had no transportation yet again. The next day, I rounded up someone with a tow truck and got the car towed to my shop. I was back to driving the old doctor's truck again.

A friend of mine who was a mechanic helped me put a used transmission in the car. I had gotten it from Rhinehart's, and it took us a couple of nights to complete the job. Finally, I was back on the road again in my old Buick.

I was still working on the old guy's truck and doing some repairs for Rhinehart. Occasionally, I would get a small customer job off the street, but I was still barely staying afloat.

Shortly after the transmission fiasco with the Buick, things began to turn around for me. I was diligently studying my *Power of Positive Thinking* book, applying all the best practices, and more and more customers were beginning to hear about my shop. The comments were positive about the quality of work I was doing, and customers were referring me to their friends.

Business improved to the point where I didn't have to depend on the cars from Ray Rhinehart to make ends meet. I still needed his equipment at the shop; I just didn't need his work any longer. Things were going OK.

One day, I asked Ray if he'd sell me the equipment. He said he would; he wanted $3,000 for it. I called my dad and told him what I was doing and that I needed $3,000. My dad thought it was a good idea and he was a smart guy. Instead of using his cash, he went to the bank, told his banker what he was going to do, and took out a loan.

He told the banker, "I want you to set it up on a 24- or 36-month note. I'm going to tell Larry what the payment is and where to send it each month. If there is ever a month you don't get the payment from Larry, you call me, and I will come over here and pay off the loan."

The payment was about $120 a month. I was thrilled to pay Ray Rhinehart and be done with renting his equipment. I think Ray gained a level of respect for me because I made the business work. He never thought I would be able to do it without him. I don't know who he found to do his grunt work after that, but I was thankful it was no longer me.

With business having picked up, I was at the point where I needed someone to help me. I spread the word that I wanted to hire someone. Soon after, a long-haired guy pulled up at the shop one day smoking a cigarette. He looked like he'd walked right out of Woodstock. He said, "Hey, man. I'm Jeff Young. I hear you need some help," and shook my hand. He seemed to be a very nice guy.

Jeff was an experienced paint and body-repair technician, so I hired him. His wife was a little bit of an odd hippie girl, but well spoken. She had an office job somewhere in town. Upon meeting her, I realized she was a little sharper than I had expected Jeff's wife to be. Jeff was happy as long as he could pay the rent on their modest house and buy his cigarettes and beer. He was a great guy, and he worked out well.

I found out early on that I could trust Jeff with anything. If I had to leave for three or four hours, Jeff would handle whatever came up at the shop. He wouldn't leave until l I got back. He was a caretaker.

Jeff and I were both working on cars and were beginning to get more and more business. I had a little more money in my bank account, and things were beginning to turn. With steady money coming in, I was paying bills and paying Jeff at the end of each week. If there was any money left over, then life was great.

It just so happened that Jeff drove a 1969 Pontiac Firebird, just like the one I had auctioned off months earlier to pay my rent. I missed that car a lot.

I can't remember what color his car was, but it had a blue front fender and a blue bumper header panel across the front. It had been in an accident, and he or somebody else had just put a used fender and a used header panel on it. They didn't even paint it. It didn't look great, but Jeff was more of a fanatic about cars running well. He was much more concerned about the engine than he was the body, and that car ran perfectly. It had the exact same engine and interior I'd had in my Firebird. The interior was in great shape, but it needed carpet.

I don't remember the terms of the deal, but I bought that car from Jeff. I was still driving my Buick but badly needed an upgrade. The body of the Firebird needed a lot of work. I would stay at the shop each night and work on it until 10:00 or 11:00 p.m. I fixed up the Firebird, painted it the exact color of the one I had before, and took it to an interior shop to have new carpet installed. When it was finished, the car looked exactly like my previous Firebird. In fact, when I drove the car home to visit my parents, they never realized it wasn't the same car. Dad asked, "Hey, how's your car doing?"

I said, "Car's doing great." I was thrilled that I was able to replace my old car.

By this time, Ted Powers, the manager at Higginbotham Chevrolet Oldsmobile and my previous boss, had left the dealership to take another job. The manager who Dennis hired to replace Ted was not doing a good job.

The body shop was struggling to turn out quality work. During this stretch of time in the late 1970s, General Motors experienced poor quality with the factory paint on their new vehicles. Many vehicles were coming off the assembly line with blemishes. Rather than repairing the paint issues at the factory, they were shipping the cars to the dealerships with the blemished paint; therefore, the repairs had to be made at the dealerships.

Dennis Higginbotham became extremely frustrated because the guys in his paint shop could not match the paint correctly when doing these repairs. One morning at the sales meeting, he told his salesmen to take the vehicles that needed repairs to my paint shop. He knew I could do the work correctly. In addition to my normal work increasing, I now frequently had one or two of Higginbotham's vehicles at my shop.

Each time a salesman would bring a car to me, he would bring a purchase order with him. These were minor repairs, typically in the $50 to $75 range, so I would hold on to the purchase orders until the end of each month and then take them to the dealership to get a check. I would give the purchase orders to the lady in accounting. She'd go to her desk, write the check, and take it to Dennis for him to sign, as was the procedure. Each month when he noticed the check was made out to me, he would always bring it out and hand it to me personally.

I knew Dennis really wanted me to go back and manage his body shop for him. Each time he brought me a check, it was another opportunity for him to see how my business was going and to see if there were any signs of me wanting to return to the dealership. Typically, we would engage in some small talk, I would thank him for his business, and then I'd head back to my shop.

9

I FINALLY GET MY DREAM CAR

In addition to my regular business, I began buying a few inexpensive, damaged cars that I would repair and sell. I soon realized the best place to find these cars was at dealerships, where they had been traded in on newer vehicles.

However, I had to have an auto-dealer license to purchase these vehicles from the dealers. I researched the requirements for a Florida dealer's license and, to my surprise, found it was pretty simple. I sent in the application and processing fee to the state, and about thirty days later, I received my license. This opened the door for me to buy vehicles from many places I previously could not.

Now that I was buying more and more damaged vehicles to repair, I needed another technician. I hired a local, experienced body technician named David Mitchum.

I also hired a helper. So now, Jeff, David and I were doing the repair work, while the helper kept the shop clean and ran errands.

There was an auto auction in Sadisco, Florida, where I began buying damaged vehicles. When an insurance company would classify a vehicle as "a total loss," the company would pay the customer for the car and send it to this auction to reclaim some of their loss.

Unlike a traditional auction, where cars are driven through the bidding lanes, the cars in Sadisco weren't drivable. The cars were lined up neatly in a mowed field by row number. The auction had an old school bus with one side cut out and removed, and the seats had been removed and reinstalled to face out the open side. The auctioneer would stand at the front of the school bus next to the driver, and the driver would go down the rows, stopping at each car. The auctioneer would call out the car's year, model, and miles, and the bidding would begin. The highest bidder got the car. Then the bus would roll on to the next car, and the process would start all over.

I would always get to the auction about two hours early. I'd walk around the field and identify vehicles that might interest me. Because of my experience, I could arrive at a pretty close estimate of what it would cost me to repair a vehicle. I'd determine the maximum I was willing to pay for a car. Many of these cars were relatively new.

Once, I purchased a 1978 Buick LeSabre with the factory window sticker still on it; it had only fifty-four miles on the odometer. It was a brand-new car owned by a dealership, and it had been involved in an accident when a salesman was with a customer on a test drive. It had major damage to the left side. This was just one of several cars I purchased from Sadisco and then repaired and resold at the shop.

Dennis Higginbotham's father, Bob, had recently retired from the Birmingham, Alabama Police Department and moved to New Smyrna Beach with his wife.

With free time on his hands, he would help around the dealership with odd jobs. One of them was bringing the cars from the dealership to my body shop for the warranty paint repairs. Bob noticed the Buick LeSabre and fell in love with it. He began dropping by the dealership daily, even if he didn't have a car to bring to me, so he could see how the repairs were progressing. When we completed the repairs, I sold the car to Bob.

In 1977, Ford made a major body-style change to the Thunderbird. It was a much sleeker, sportier car than the previous model and was one of the most popular cars from 1977 to 1979. I wanted a new Ford T-Bird in the worst way.

Ideally, I had been hoping to find one that had been wrecked that I could buy and fix. But because the model I wanted had just recently been introduced, the chance of finding a wrecked one was not very good. One day, I was in my shop working when I decided to go to the Ford dealership in Daytona and buy a new T-Bird.

I drove down to Bud Lawrence Ford in Daytona. I was young and wearing my old work clothes at the time. The four or five salesmen standing outside didn't pay any attention to me as I walked across the lot to where the new T-Birds were. They seemed more interested in smoking their cigarettes and talking than in helping me. I walked over to the T-Birds and saw some new 1979 models that had just arrived, along with a nice supply of 1978 models. I assumed I would be able to get the best deal on one of the remaining 1978 models, so I spent about twenty minutes looking at them. The salesmen remained in front of the building, just looking at me. I assumed they thought I was just a broke kid who was only dreaming of buying a new car.

After I found the car I liked, I walked over to the salesmen and said, "Does anyone want to sell me a new T-Bird?"

One of the sloppy-looking salesmen dropped his cigarette and said, "Yeah, man, how many do you want to buy?"

The others got a laugh from his remark.

I said, "Only one, but if that's not enough for you, I'll get one of your buddies to help me."

He followed me over to the car. I can't remember the asking price of the car now, but I offered $7,200. I said, "I want to buy this one. I have a dealer's license, so I don't need a tag, and I'm not going to pay sales tax. I'll bring you a check for $7,200 for the car tomorrow."

The salesman paused. I think he was a little surprised by the way I took control. This was the exact opposite of what customers typically did. Back in those days, salespeople were taught to always maintain control of the customer. I had immediately taken control of him and the situation. He said he would need to ask his manager about the price and about my paying no sales tax. He came back to me in about fifteen minutes and said his manager approved the deal. I left to secure my financing. I'm sure he thought he would never see me again.

I went straight to Southeast Bank, my bank in New Smyrna. Sam Gillam was the loan officer. I had banked with them since opening my shop and had established a nice relationship with him. I took Sam a copy of the sales order from the dealership and asked if he would finance the car. Sam said he would and said I could pick up the check in the morning.

In the early afternoon the following day, I left my shop and went back to the bank to get the check. I had one of my workers drive me to Daytona and drop me off at the Ford dealership. I paid for the car and drove back to my shop. The car was beautiful; it was gray. It was the first brand-new car I had owned since I'd bought my 1974 Firebird Formula 400.

Business was going well. I was still repairing damaged cars and selling them. I had two cars that were ready to sell, and I was going to take them to the Sanford Auto Auction for their Tuesday-night sale. Blake Simmons worked for his father at Preston's Exxon in New Smyrna. Preston not only owned the gas station on US 1 but also had one of the major 24-hour wrecker services in town. Blake was one or two years younger than me. We had become good friends. Another employee was Luther. I asked Blake and Luther to drive the two cars to Sanford for the Tuesday-night sale, and I followed in my new T-Bird.

My cars were in line to run early during the auction. I sold them both for a good price. The auction did the final sales transactions and exchanged checks only at the end of the sale, after all the cars had gone through the bidding lanes. I knew we had at least two more hours before the sale would be over and I could get paid. Rather than stand around at the auction, I suggested we go to a local sports bar about twenty minutes away to get something to eat.

We went to the sports bar, ate, and had one beer each. We left the sports bar and were traveling down Hwy. 17-92, back toward the auction, when this real big guy in an old Chevy Nova stopped next to us at the traffic light. This guy was obviously high on something. He had big hair that went everywhere. His music was very loud, and he was yelling something. We just sat there looking at him until the light changed. When we drove off, he stayed close beside us. If I slowed, he slowed. When I would speed up, he would as well.

He then began moving his car over into my lane. I was driving my new T-Bird with less than one thousand miles on it. I hadn't even made the first payment yet. He got so far into my lane a couple times that I had to drive off the side of the road to avoid him. By then, I was upset and yelling at him. He continued this erratic driving while laughing more and more.

I looked in my rearview mirror and saw a car coming down 17-92 behind us with blue lights flashing. I slowed down, and the crazy guy got in front of me. The police officer passed me and stopped the big guy. I told Blake and Luther that I was glad to have a cop around at the right time. We kept driving toward the auction, and about 30 seconds later, I saw another police car coming down the highway behind us. This cop pulled me over, so I stopped, rolled down the window, and handed him my driver's license.

He went back to his patrol car for a few minutes, and when he came back, he told me to turn around and drive to where the big guy's car was parked. I assumed he wanted me to tell him the entire story. We got back to where the big guy was, and the two police officers started talking. The other driver was already in the backseat of the other officer's car.

The police officer who pulled me over said the big guy told them we were playing "chicken." Chicken is a dangerous game drivers play when they are trying to make each other wreck. Obviously, the guy was blown away, stoned, high, or something, because he was telling the police he was playing a game with a motor vehicle that would get him arrested. I said to the cop who stopped me, "Officer, I'm driving a brand-new car with less than one thousand miles on it. Do you really think I'm playing chicken?"

I heard the other officer say to the one talking to me that I probably didn't care because my dad most likely bought me the car.

This remark fired me up, and I made the stupid comment, "Just because a Seminole County Sheriff Deputy can't afford a new car doesn't mean I can't."

This was a big mistake. After the two police officers talked a bit more, they told me they were arresting me for careless and reckless driving.

The cop who pulled me over put me in the back of his patrol car. Blake and Luther were still waiting in my car. I asked the police office what to do about my car sitting on the side of the highway. He said, sarcastically, that I could have one of the guys in the car drive it to the police station, or he could have it towed and impounded. My choice. I told him the guys would follow us.

The officer then sped off at a high rate of speed. There was no reason for this because I was calm and confined in the backseat of his car. He was in total control. I asked him to slow down so Blake could keep up. Blake had no idea what police station we were headed to, and we were in a strange town. The officer continued his fast driving.

Finally, I said, "I see what you're doing. You want my friend to have to speed to keep up and then you can have one of your buddies pull him over as well."

He told me to shut up. When we arrived at the police station, he put me in a holding cell for more than thirty minutes. He came back later and said, "Hey, hotshot, it's going to be a little tougher for you to get out of jail tonight than you thought."

I said, "What do you mean?"

He said, "I'm arresting you for aggravated assault with a motor vehicle. The bail will be $5,250."

I looked at the cop and said, "You're sick."

I used my one phone call to call a local bail bondsman. I answered the questions he asked. He said the 10 percent fee for posting my bail would be $525 and asked if I had that much money on me. Although I had only about a hundred dollars on me, I paused for a second and then said yes. I told him he would see a new gray Ford T-Bird when he pulled into the parking lot, and I had $1,000 in the glove box (which I did not). He said he would be there in about an hour.

When someone is arrested, the officer or staff takes your personal items and holds them in an envelope at the booking desk. I learned this from my DUI charge when my tire was shot out years before. I assumed that when the bondsman arrived, he would ask the jailer if there was $525 in my envelope, and when he saw less than $100, he would simply leave.

I was escorted to a big holding cell with probably twenty men in it. When the jailer slid the door open, he told me to find a place to sit because when the door closed, it would be pretty dark. My cellmates looked rough, and I wasn't sure if the big guy from the highway incident was in there or not because I didn't have time to see everyone before the officer closed the door.

Two metal picnic tables sat in the middle of the big cell. They were big and heavy, and the benches were welded to them on each side. Right when the jailer was closing the door, I slid under one of those big tables. I sat there under the table, not making a noise, until that door opened again and the jailer called my name. Man, I bounced out from under that table and rushed through the open door.

When he took me back downstairs, a woman was standing there holding some paperwork. She was maybe in her mid-to-late fifties. She looked just like a mom. She worked for the bondsman, and it was her job to get me out of jail. When I signed the paperwork, she said, "I saw the T-Bird in the parking lot. You do have cash in the glove box to cover my $525 fee, correct?"

I said, "Yes, ma'am."

Blake and Luther were asleep in the little lobby of the jail. Luther was asleep on a small sofa and Blake on the floor. I woke them, and we all four walked outside. As we approached my car, I turned to the lady and said, "Ma'am, I don't have any money in the glove box."

She stopped dead in her tracks and said, "What?!"

I repeated it and then followed up by saying, "You have two choices. One, give me the address of your office and the time to be there in the morning with the $525. Or two, I'm assuming you have a firearm in that big purse on your shoulder. You can shoot me. I'm not going back in that jail."

She gave me the address of her office and said she would be there at 8:30 a.m. the next day, and her boss would be there at 9:00 a.m. She went on to say that if she didn't have that money before he got there, she would be fired. I assured her not to be concerned about it. I always kept some cash at my house.

Back at home, I took a shower and got a couple of hours of sleep. I walked into her office at 8:40 and dropped $525 on her desk. I thought she was going to hug me. Then I said, "Please point me in the direction of the best attorney in town. I need to get out of this bogus charge." She gave me his name and directions.

It was a couple minutes after 9:00 a.m. when I walked into his office; his assistant had just arrived, and I asked to speak with the attorney. She said he would be in court until 11:00, but I was welcome to wait on him. I sat there in the reception area for two hours, thinking about the events of the previous night. When the attorney arrived, he glanced over at me for a second and stopped to talk to her. I assumed he was asking what I wanted. He walked into his office, and a few minutes later, she told me I could go in to speak with him.

I told him exactly how the evening unfolded. I even told him about my comment to the cops that probably landed me in jail. He got a little laugh from this. He asked a few questions and then said for me to give him a $500 retainer fee, and he would get started on the case. He would call me when he needed more money. I dropped $500 on his desk and left. In less than three hours that morning, I had gone through $1,025, which was a lot of money in 1978.

Since I walked out of that attorney's office almost forty-five years ago, I have never heard from him. I'm thinking he earned the $500 for about fifteen minutes of work. I'm sure he called the sheriff or the county prosecutor and suggested they drop these unrealistic, trumped-up charges this renegade cop had placed against me because of my sarcastic comment.

Over the years, I have learned from attorneys and law-enforcement officials I have met that although these guys may be on different sides, they have respect for each other and really work well together behind closed doors.

10

BACK TO WORK FOR DENNIS

One fall day, I received a form letter in the mail from the Florida Department of Motor Vehicles that was sent to all auto dealers. The message was informing us that as of January 1, 1979, any vehicle purchased that had been classified as a total loss would be issued a "rebuilt" title, also known as a "branded title."

Up until then, totaled vehicles had come with their original titles, known as "clean titles." In other words, nothing on the title indicated the vehicle had been wrecked and rebuilt, and sellers were not required to disclose this. It appeared, upon receiving this letter, that my business model was about to change significantly. Not only would I have to disclose all prior damage, but banks were not going to finance cars with rebuilt titles for buyers. The value of rebuilt vehicles would plummet.

I still had three or four vehicles in my shop that I had bought previously, so I had enough work for the guys to do until the end of the year while I contemplated my next move.

Dennis Higginbotham called me one day from his dealership and asked if I would come by to see him. Ironically, this was only a few days after I received the letter from the state. I met him at his office. He asked if I would be interested in leasing his body shop from him. The question did pique my interest, so I asked him to give me the details.

He said, "The body shop would keep its current name, and the public will still come here to get estimates and repairs. You'll still perform the warranty work. You'll just pay me a flat monthly fee for leasing it, and you'll keep the proceeds. Basically, I'm getting out of the paint and body business. It would be your business, just as your body shop is now."

I told him I had interest in discussing it in greater detail when he gathered more information. I left it at that. I knew the Chevrolet Oldsmobile sign out front would bring me a lot of work.

Two weeks later, Dennis called and asked me to meet with him again. He said, "I have more details concerning the lease thing. I have confirmed it can be done and is not an uncommon concept. It will take some time, though, because attorneys and CPAs will need to be involved, and a contract will need to be created. Here's what I'd like to do. I'd like for you to begin working here as soon as you can. I realize most of the work you're doing currently is on your own vehicles, and you have a couple of body guys there working for you. They could continue working for you at the shop, and you could begin here as soon as possible. It will most likely take three or four months for us to get the lease paperwork put together, so in the meantime, you would be a Higginbotham Chevrolet Oldsmobile employee."

I accepted his offer.

I really didn't have interest in managing his paint and body shop; however, I didn't mind doing it for a short period until it became my business. While we waited on the lease process to be completed, Dennis paid me $300 a week, plus 10 percent of net profit of the paint and body shop. He also provided me a company vehicle. I would go to the dealership each day, and Jeff and Dave continued finishing up the work at my shop. They had about ninety days of work to do. I'd stop by after work and check on them.

My first day was on a Thursday. When I arrived at the dealership, I couldn't believe how filthy and disorganized the shop was. I couldn't wait for the weekend to come because the shop was closed on Saturdays and Sundays. On Saturday morning, I arrived at daybreak with a truck I borrowed from a friend. I spent both days hauling off multiple truckloads of trash, old paint, damaged parts, old scraps, and other debris. I then reorganized the shop and cleaned it from top to bottom. When my workers arrived Monday morning, they knew there was a new sheriff in town. They almost seemed uncomfortable in such a clean, organized environment.

I spent most of the first month redoing work on vehicles that had not previously been done properly. Also, my predecessor did not keep an appointment log, so I had no idea what was scheduled to come in each day. I was working blind. I would open the doors in the morning and wait to see who would arrive. It was usually customers whose cars we had already repaired, but not properly. In the business, it's known as a "comeback." Technicians despise comebacks because they know they have to stop what they're doing and redo work they've already been paid to do. Although the technicians understood this is how it worked, they still ranted and raved when this happened and complained about having to do the job for nothing.

My response was, "I'm sorry. I regret you feel this way, but you should have done the job properly the first time."

We had so many comebacks that I was concerned a couple of the guys were going to quit. Because of the poor quality of the work, they all probably needed to be fired anyway, but I didn't have anyone to replace them at the time. In an effort to reduce the pain, I ended up staying at the shop after hours at night, doing some of the comeback repairs myself.

After the first month, I had most of the comebacks out of the way and was able to begin scheduling good, revenue-generating work.

One day, I noticed the office manager, Sandy Kennedy, walking around handing the other managers their monthly bonus checks. She didn't bring me one. I went to her office and said, "Hey, Sandy, I didn't get a check."

She replied, "You didn't get a check because your department didn't make any money. Larry, your department never makes money."

I guess she noticed the shocked look on my face because she stood up and closed her door. She asked me to have a seat. She pulled out a copy of the paint and body shop financial statement from the previous month and began a 30-minute tutorial in accounting on how to generate a profit in your department. This was my very first introduction to how the numbers worked. I was a good repair technician, I was good with my employees, I was good with customers, and I understood the auto repair processes as well as most, but this was my first lesson in business.

The next month, I got a check.

At the beginning of each month, we would have a managers' meeting to review the previous month's performance. We were crowded in Dennis's modest office one morning for the meeting, and he reached behind his desk and pulled out a bottle of champagne. He gave each of us a small plastic cup of it and announced we were celebrating the fact it was the first month since he had owned the dealership that the paint and body shop had made a profit! To the best of my knowledge, we never lost money again during my tenure.

Ironically, after we began making a profit, he never brought up the lease option again. I didn't, either. I just remained an employee.

I developed a simple process that ensured we always had plenty of work in the body shop.

Back when working for Andy Barefoot in Raleigh, I had noticed that customers would come in throughout the day asking for an estimate on their vehicle. Andy would stop what he was doing, grab his estimate pad, and go outside to write an estimate on the car. It might have taken ten minutes if it was minor or an hour if there was major damage. Regardless, he would total up the estimate and give the customer a copy. Then he would say, "Here you go. Let me know if we can help you." The customer would thank him and walk out the door.

I noticed when arriving at Dennis's that Ted Powers would do the exact same thing. Studying both men doing this, I realized that I rarely saw those customers bring their cars back to the body shop for the repairs. Basically, these two managers were spending a lot of time writing estimates, with no return. What customers didn't realize is that, in most cases, the insurance companies write their own estimates. I also learned that most people who came in for an estimate had never been in an auto accident before and had no idea how the system worked. They simply thought they needed an estimate before contacting their insurance company.

My practice was that, when someone would bring their vehicle in, I'd write them an estimate. Even though I knew the insurance adjuster was going to write their own estimate, I spent the time writing the estimate so I could spend time with the customer. When I finished, I would explain to customers what to expect next. I'd ask them questions pertaining to who was at fault in the accident and then explain the different regulations insurance companies have. I educated them and offered to handle all the details with their insurance company. The customers were amazed at how well I handled all the details for them. As I would go through my little process, I could see the anxiety vanish from their faces.

This additional time I spent with them paid huge dividends.

Oddly enough, about half the insurance claims at the dealership were with State Farm. The adjuster for State Farm who handled New Smyrna Beach was Dick Martin. I knew Dick well and had a great working relationship with him from my own body-shop days. Dick and I had mutual respect. I liked Dick because he sent me a lot of work, and Dick liked me because I did his job for him. Adjusters don't make a lot of money, and they have a thankless job. My goal was to make his job as easy as possible. Instead of Dick coming to the dealership in his required dress clothes, climbing around and under vehicles, spending time writing detailed estimates, and taking Polaroid pictures for the file, I would do these things in advance. He could simply show up, get the file, and head to his next appointment.

State Farm required their adjusters to write all estimates personally on a State Farm appraisal form. Dick would leave with my estimate, and in a couple of days, I would receive his estimate in the mail. It would be my estimate rewritten on a State Farm appraisal form. He loved doing business with me! The insurance companies assigned the adjusters their jobs daily. They allowed about an hour and a half for each stop. Dick would be at the dealership for about fifteen minutes. He had a lot of free time on his hands.

Because of the way I assisted him, he would send customers my way as often as he could. I use him as an example because he provided about 50 percent of our insurance business.

However, I provided this level of service for all insurance adjusters. Allstate Insurance Company had two young female adjusters. They always came out wearing their nice skirts or dresses. I would have all the dirty work done for them by the time they arrived. They sent me tons of business.

Obviously, other shop managers didn't do this because I always had the busiest shop in the area. This best practice created such an increase in business that we had to build an addition to the paint and body shop.

I had some knowledge of the wrecker and towing business. Andy had a wrecker service when I worked for him in Raleigh. I was ready to take our business to the next level, and I pitched Dennis on getting into the wrecker service business. I explained that we were getting the folks who had been in an accident and came to us for an estimate, but how about the people who were leaving their houses to go to work or shopping and had no idea they would be in an accident in a couple hours? If you have the proper equipment and open a 24-hour wrecker service, you can apply to get on the towing rotation for the local police department, sheriff's department, and Highway Patrol. There were three 24-hour wrecker services in town.

I presented my case to Dennis for us to become the fourth. In addition to the actual towing and recovery fee, we would pick up a daily storage fee for each day a wrecked vehicle sat at the shop, but more importantly, we would have many more repair opportunities.

Dennis agreed to let me buy a class B wrecker, which would qualify for all the police agencies. I handled it all. I found and bought the wrecker, had it lettered up to meet the requirements, and completed the application process, and we were on the rotation. The only catch, according to Dennis, was that I had to run the service myself at nights and weekends for the first ninety days. Then, if we were successful, we could hire a night and weekend driver. The business took off, and in a year, I was buying our second wrecker. I had a full-time wrecker driver for the daytime and a full-time night driver. If we got called to a bad accident that required multiple wreckers, the nighttime guy would call me, and I would assist him. The additional repair work that the wrecker service brought us was great. We immediately brought that addition we had built to the shop to capacity.

Back during those years, a person could own multiple dealerships but could be the dealer principal of only one dealership. That's not the case today. There are plenty of mega-dealers who are the dealer principals for all their auto dealerships.

While Dennis was running the small dealership in New Smyrna, he wanted to purchase a larger dealership in Daytona Beach, about twenty-five miles away. It was named Sunrise Toyota Oldsmobile. He wanted to have his office there and run this store himself because it was a larger dealership.

However, if he was going to be the dealer principal at the new dealership, the New Smyrna dealership would require another dealer principal. It just so happened that his cousin, Dick Higginbotham, was a mid-level executive with Chevrolet Motor Company. Although he had never worked in a car dealership, he'd always wanted to be in the retail car business. Dennis offered this opportunity to Dick, who purchased 25 percent of Higginbotham Chevrolet Oldsmobile and became the dealer principal. Dennis was still the primary stockholder, but Dick was on record as the dealer.

One day while I was working at the Chevy Olds dealership, Dennis called and said, "Hey, Larry, I'd like for you to run the body shop here in Daytona."

It was a much bigger shop with greater opportunity, and the guy currently running it was in over his head. Dennis asked me to go talk to Dick about it. Dick gave me his blessing to make the move, and I became the body shop manager of Sunrise Toyota Oldsmobile.

When I was the body shop manager there, my direct supervisor was the Service Director, Larry Hadaway. I'd been there for about a year when Larry submitted a letter of resignation to Dennis. One day, Dennis called me into his office, showed me the letter, and said he wanted me to take Larry's job. My new position had me responsible for the Service Department, Parts Department, and paint and body shop. The three managers of these departments reported to me.

I soon realized that many of the best practices I'd used when running the body shop would apply nicely to all the departments. The combination of my experience and training that Dennis provided put me on a quick path to success as Service Director.

Although I had no formal education, Dennis invested heavily in my training. At the time, General Motors offered a two-year business class that was held at various locations around the country. For the southeastern part of the country, it was held at Oglethorpe University in Atlanta, Georgia. I would go to classes there for one week per quarter. They were taught by accredited professors in a manner specifically designed for car dealership management. In the weeks between classes, we would do ongoing correspondence work with the school. I found this to be excellent training for my current position and future positions.

It was 1984 now, and Dennis had just built a new state-of-the-art dealership on "car row" in Daytona Beach to move the Toyota Oldsmobile dealership into. We were getting settled into the new facility as I was getting settled into my new position.

Shortly after I became the Service Director at the Toyota Oldsmobile dealership, the Warranty Administrator quit. This is a clerical position that requires experience. The Warranty Administrator prepared and submitted warranty repair claims to Toyota and Oldsmobile for reimbursement. I hired a lady with experience. She had worked for the Chevrolet dealership next door to our dealership for several years, although it had been a few years prior. She provided great references. She was legally blind. I knew this when I hired her. She got a ride to work every day with a friend. She could get around fine and worked with a big magnifying glass. I saw that her disability would not cause a problem with her performing her duties.

From the very beginning, though, she struggled. I was somewhat surprised that someone with her experience would be having such a hard time. By the way, the Chevrolet dealership she had previously worked for was a bigger dealership than ours. Her workload there would have been greater. After several talks about her poor performance, I had no choice but to replace her. During the termination meeting, she claimed that I was terminating her because of her disability. She went on to tell me that she was part of a national organization that stood up against employers who unjustly terminated disabled employees. I thought it was a little odd that she spoke about this as long as she did. I saw a side of her that day that I'd not before seen. It was very strange.

About two weeks later, I received a letter from the Labor Board notifying me of a hearing that I was required to attend. Due to the sensitive nature of the claim, Dennis suggested I take our company attorney, Jerry Wells, to the hearing with me. I brought him up to speed on the details while making the 30-minute drive to the hearing. There were four attendees: the ex-employee, Sally; a hearing officer; Jerry; and me. After the hour-long hearing, we were found of no wrongdoing. Sally stared at me as we left. She was very upset and mad.

That night at about 11:00 p.m., I received a phone call. I was a little groggy from having been woken up when I answered. A male voice said, "I am a detective with the Los Angeles Police Department, and we are on our way to get you." When he ended the call with no further details, I assumed it was a prank.

A couple days later, I received a letter at my house that was postmarked Flushing, New York. The letter said I needed to sleep with one eye open because my days were numbered. I wondered if this was the end for me. I was very uncomfortable about the entire situation.

I had legally purchased a .38 Special handgun when I was in my early twenties and always kept it in my nightstand drawer. The next morning when I went to work, I put it in my car to take with me. The following evening when I got home, I found a sympathy card in the mail postmarked Champaign, Illinois. It said, "Sorry for your recent loss. You are next. We will be there soon."

The next day, I took the letter and card to the local office of the FBI in Daytona Beach. I told them about the Warranty Administrator. They asked if I knew of anyone else who may have an axe to grind with me, and I said no. I never heard back from the FBI. This series of events continued to bother me and was consuming my thoughts. I continued to think Sally was behind the harassment.

One evening, before I left work, I pulled Sally's employment application and got her home phone number and called her. She answered and was very cordial during our short conversation. I told her that an automobile technician had applied for a job with us a few days earlier and had listed her as a reference since he had worked at the same Chevrolet dealership as she had a few years prior. I told her I couldn't remember his last name, but his first name was David. I asked if she remembered him. She thought for a couple minutes and said, "I don't think this name rings a bell."

I went on to tell her he had mentioned during the interview that he wouldn't be able to start work for a few weeks because he was traveling. He was going to Flushing, New York, and then was going to spend a few days in Champaign, Illinois, and then wrap up his trip in Los Angeles.

There was silence on the phone for a few seconds. Sally then said, "Gosh, Larry. I'm sorry. Again, this name doesn't ring a bell, and I can't think of who the applicant may be."

I thanked her for her time and hung up the phone. Sally now knew that I suspected her. There was no David. I had made the entire story up but included the specific addresses from the letter and card to let her know I was tying her to the harassment. Obviously, she understood the purpose of my call because I received no further threatening correspondence.

11

CHARLES "HAYDEN" BYRD

Shortly after I moved to New Smyrna Beach, I met a wonderful man by the name of Hayden Byrd. Hayden and I bought gas at the same station, and I would frequently see him there talking to Preston, the owner. Back then, gas stations did not have convenience stores. They only sold gas and performed maintenance repairs on vehicles. All gas stations had a mechanic on staff. Regular customers would stop by to get gas and frequently go inside for a few minutes. Sometimes they would buy a drink from the soda machine and visit with the owner or staff for a bit.

This was how Preston's Exxon was, and this was how I got to know Hayden. He was a banker at the bank next door. He was also from North Carolina, so we had an immediate bond. Hayden was about twenty years older than me. I think he saw much of his younger self in me. He became a good friend and mentor.

In 1979, I began dating a young lady named Kristie after she was hired at the Chevy Olds dealership. What attracted me to her was that she was a very happy-go-lucky person. That's how we both were when we dated. In 1980, as Hayden's and my friendship continued to grow, he knew I was renting a duplex and that Kristie and I had decided to get married. He called one day and said, "Isn't it about time you bought a house?"

Mortgage rates had ballooned to 18 percent at the time. Naturally, home sales had come to a screeching halt because of this. Hayden's bank had financed the construction of eight small homes in a neighborhood about five minutes from the dealership. Unfortunately, the bank had to foreclose on the builder because his houses weren't selling. Hayden told me about the builder's misfortune and told me to go look at the houses and pick the one I liked. I said, "That would be great, but I don't have the money to buy a house." He told me he thought the interest rates would drop within the next couple of months, which would make it more affordable, and we'd work out the details later.

I drove over and saw the houses. Two were on a paved road, and six were on a dirt road. There were two styles; one was a little bigger than the other. I chose the bigger of the two on the paved road. Hayden didn't want to write my loan at 18 percent and suggested that I move into the house and begin setting it up with furniture and other things I may need. We would close in two or three months in anticipation of the rates dropping.

He called about three months later and said, "The rates have dropped to fourteen percent. Unfortunately, I don't see them dropping more in the near future. We need to close on your house." He said the payment would be $400 a month, including home insurance and property tax payments. While this amount was a lot higher than my current rent of $155 at the duplex, it still fell within my budget. He asked me to be at his office the next day at 3:00.

When I arrived the following day, he told me to go into the office where the closing would be held. He had reviewed the documents for accuracy and said, "All you need to do is sign where the agent tells you and give her twelve hundred dollars."

I froze and said, "Hayden, I don't have twelve hundred dollars."

He stood up with a sarcastic smile and giggled. He said, "I knew you didn't. I just wanted to see the look on your face." He reached into his pocket, took out twelve $100 bills, and dropped them on the desk. He said, "Take this and go close on your house." I told him that I didn't know when I could pay him back. Hayden said, "I don't care if you ever pay me. You're about to get married. You need to own a home."

I took the $1,200 and went to sign the papers. Paying him back was priority number one for me. I think I had him paid back within ninety days!

Everyone needs a Hayden Byrd in his or her life.

Kristie and I married in the late summer of 1980. Shortly thereafter, I began to change. I turned into my dad. I felt it was time to grow up and be accountable for the responsibilities I had. As a result, I wasn't the happy-go-lucky guy I had been previously. Kristie and I had much different views of what marriage should be like, and we hadn't discussed this at all before marrying.

After about eighteen months, she left and went back to the life she had before we were married. We divorced on the day of our second anniversary in 1982. I paid Kristie for half the equity we had in the house and became the sole owner. As I look back today, I don't blame her for leaving. I was making the decision that her life was going to change without discussing it with her. My mistake.

After my divorce, I became immersed in my work for the next few years. Although I occasionally dated, my primary focus was my career. Things were going well, and I began to feel that I had a good future in the car business. Working hard and learning all I could became my priority.

In 1985, I began to date Gayle Newman, a cashier at the Toyota Oldsmobile dealership. She had been married previously, also for a short period, to a guy who was a little older. After they divorced, Gayle moved back in with her mom and dad and was living there when we began to date. Several months later, the relationship became serious, and she moved in with me. About eighteen months later, in the fall of 1986, we married.

Prior to us marrying, we had decided to buy a piece of property and build a new house at Sugar Mill Country Club in New Smyrna. By that time, I was doing well, making decent money, and could afford a nicer home. On the weekends, we would ride around to different developments, looking at new houses to get ideas. One day we went to an open house in Spruce Creek Country Club in Daytona Beach. We saw a home that had just been completed that we really liked. We decided we wanted to build this exact house on our lot in Sugar Mill. It had three bedrooms and two bathrooms—nothing big and fancy, but it was a nice home. I found out who the builder was and called him the next week to ask if he would sell me the plans to the house.

He said, "No, but I'll build the house for you."

I said, "No thanks, I'll find something else."

The next Sunday, we went back by the house. There was no "open house" that day, but the house was unlocked. We went in, and I sketched out a rough draft of the house and rooms on a legal pad. Gayle and I measured the rooms, as well as the exterior dimensions. After we left, I bought a pad of drafting paper and later at home drew the house to scale. I took the drawing to a draftsman, and he created the architect's blueprint.

My banker buddy, Hayden, knew everybody in town. I called to tell him I'd bought a lot out in Sugar Mill Country Club and wanted to build a house. I asked who he would recommend to build it. Hayden had a friend who had been a builder for a long time and built a lot of houses in New Smyrna Beach. The builder's son had been working with him since he was a kid. The son had just gotten his contractor's license the previous month. Hayden wanted the son to get a couple of new houses under his belt before he went out on his own. Hayden worked out a deal with his son to build my house at his cost, and then I would just pay him a flat fee. I don't remember what the fee was, but it was incredibly cheap.

I got a construction loan from Hayden's bank. At various phases of construction, I would get draws so the builder's son could pay his subcontractors. Hayden would go out to inspect the progress and make sure the construction was being done properly. The kid worked hard on the job. I think Hayden often reminded him that I was a good friend of his and that he needed to do a great job. Sometimes on Friday afternoons, I would take a case of cold beer out to the crew at the home site. I wanted them to know I appreciated their hard work.

Once the house was built, I converted the construction loan into a home loan and rolled the taxes and homeowner's insurance into the payment, which was $1,100 a month. That was a big house payment in 1985. Gayle wasn't making a lot of money in her office job, but I was still working at the Toyota Oldsmobile dealership and doing well as the Service Director, so we were doing fine.

As time went on, Gayle decided she wanted to do something other than clerical work in an office. She left her job at the dealership and went into floral design. She picked it up quickly and worked for a couple of different local florists. Floral design seemed to be a good fit for her. We were enjoying our new home.

12

JOE GETS DEEP-SIXED

Dennis and I went to lunch quite often. I learned a lot from him during these meals. One day he said, "My plan is to buy two or three more car dealerships. You've done very well in the various positions you've held. I need you to learn the sales operation and learn more about the business operations of the dealership. I think I can develop you into a good dealership operator."

The General Manager at the dealership had recently resigned, and Dennis was looking for a replacement. He hired a guy named Joe Smith. Joe had operated a Ford dealership in Little Rock, Arkansas. He had an MBA from University of Arkansas and was a great guy, but he was not a mover and a shaker. The dealership he had operated in Little Rock must have been a sleeper because Joe was a sleeper. Everybody liked him, but he didn't hold anyone accountable.

As a lifelong student of people, it didn't take me long to realize Joe wasn't going to make it.

While he lasted longer than I thought he would, all the horsepower actually came from Dennis, and I knew this. I was confused as to why Dennis let this go on for so long, but Dennis was holding on to Joe for a reason. He would terminate Joe when he felt I was at the point where I could become the General Manager.

I didn't know this at the time. I was just working hard and patiently waiting to see where things would go. I knew Dennis wanted me to move up in the dealership at some point, so I worked hard. I made sure I was the first one there in the morning and the last one to leave in the evening. The other managers respected me because they knew I was practically living at the store. They knew I was soaking up everything about the business I could. I did not participate in any nonsense; I was working and learning.

During this period, I was working in the various sales-related departments. On weekends, I was out on the lot with salespeople, selling vehicles. During the week, I was working with one of the Sales Managers or Finance Managers. Dennis continued sending me to different training schools. I also began my second training school at Oglethorpe University in Atlanta. It was much like the first one but focused more on overall dealership operations and accounting, with emphasis on sales and finance.

If you didn't get the job done, Dennis didn't like you, and he'd let you go, no matter who you were. He would not put up with poor performance. People knew he and I were close and had a tight relationship. I worked for him for more than twenty years and was the longest-term employee he ever had. People would say Dennis had me working for him because he liked me. Dennis liked me because I got the job done.

He had just opened a new dealership in Port Richey, Florida, and went over there for a couple days to work with the new General Manager. Dick Higginbotham was Managing Partner at the Chevy Olds store, with minority ownership interest, but he had nothing to do with any of the other dealerships. He was a great guy and a good communicator. Everyone liked him.

One day while Dennis was gone to Port Richey, Dick came to the Toyota Oldsmobile dealership. He walked over to me with a big smile as always, shook my hand, and we chatted for a few minutes. As he walked off, I noticed he was headed to Joe Smith's office. I went back to what I was doing. Dick stayed in Joe's office for fifteen minutes or so. As he was leaving, he didn't stop to talk, but he did wave goodbye when he walked past me.

A couple of minutes after Dick left, Joe left his office and walked out the front door to the showroom. There was a high porch with steps leading down to the main level. He was just standing there, staring off into nowhere. A few minutes later, I walked out there and asked, "What's going on, big guy?"

He said, "I just got deep-sixed." I had never heard this term before and asked what it meant. He said, "Dick just told me that Dennis was going to make a change and didn't need me anymore. I just got fired."

Everyone has their own little quirks; I'm loaded with them. Dennis's quirk was that he had difficulty sitting down across from employees and reprimanding them, much less terminating them. When he terminated someone, he would send them a note. People called it the "poison pen letter." I don't know if he did this because he didn't like confrontation or if he was concerned the meeting would get out of hand and tempers would flare. For whatever reason, Dennis had asked Dick, who was such a professional businessman, to terminate Joe in his absence. It was late in the afternoon when it happened. Joe packed up his personal items and left the dealership. There is no notice in the car business when you get terminated. You just pack up your stuff and leave.

This was before cell phones, so Dick couldn't call Dennis to tell him the "hit" had been made. It took Dick approximately thirty minutes to get back to the Chevy Olds store in New Smyrna Beach, where he could call him. About forty-five minutes after Dick left, Dennis called the dealership to speak with me. When I picked up the phone, Dennis asked, "Hey, man. What's going on?"

I said, "Not much. Joe just left."

He said, "Yeah, man. I hated to do that, but Larry, you know it wasn't working out."

I told him I understood. He said, "Is everything else OK? How are the people acting?"

I said, "Everyone is fine. I'm not sure most of the people even know he's gone. He just loaded a box with his things and walked out the back door."

Dennis was going to be in Port Richey for two days. By the next day, everyone knew Joe was gone. Tommy

McDaniel was the new Toyota Sales Manager, and Lee Bent was the new Oldsmobile Sales Manager. They both wanted Joe's job. They were champing at the bit for it. Sales Managers always want to move up. It's just the way they're wired. They think if they can manage a sales team, they can run a dealership, but there is *so* much more to running a dealership. Jeff King was the Used Vehicle Manager, and he was a great one, but he had no interest in being a General Manager.

Dennis was back at the dealership the following day, and it was just business as usual. About lunch time, he came downstairs and said, "Let's go get something to eat."

We went to one of our usual places. As we sat there eating, talking about the dealership, I asked Dennis, "What are you going to do now that Joe's gone?"

He hesitated for a second and said, "I'm thinking about putting you in that job."

"Wow," I said. "This is a little different."

"Yeah, but I think you can do it," he said.

We talked about what we'd do and how we'd do it. He said, "I'm here to help you. If you have any questions, just ask."

Personal computers weren't around then. Most interoffice memos were handwritten. Next to the receptionist's desk were message boxes for each manager and salesperson. The very first box was labeled DDH—that was Dennis. The next box was for the General Manager, and the following boxes were for the Sales Managers and salespeople. As Maggie, the receptionist, took messages from customers calling or in-house messages from managers, she would take the message and place it in that person's box.

During the day when I'd walk past my box, I would look inside to see if there were any messages. The pink messages were typically phone calls from customers, but we would also have memos from the managers to the salespeople. That's how we communicated. Any time Dennis had to send a memo, he wrote it by hand on a small piece of paper, made copies of it on the copy machine, and then had Maggie put the message in the different boxes.

When Dennis and I got back from lunch, I didn't go into Joe's office. I didn't want to go in there. First, because he was a friend of mine, I felt bad that he had been fired, and second, it had not yet been announced that I was the new General Manager. I still wanted to work out of the small office I currently had. I didn't say anything to anybody about the conversation Dennis and I'd had at lunch.

A couple of hours later, I noticed there was a message in everyone's box. The note said, "Attention Sales Department: Effective today, Larry Hill becomes the General Manager of the dealership. He's going to do a great job. Smart guy. Y'all know Larry. Appreciate it if you give him 100 percent of your support…blah, blah, blah. Dennis, DDH." Or D, or however he signed documents.

That's how people began to realize what was happening. A few people walked up to me and said, "Hey, man, congratulations." I think Tommy and Lee both did, but I could tell they were just sick about my promotion. They both wanted the job so badly.

A few days after my promotion, Dennis finally said, "Hill, move into that office." I just didn't want to do that. Finally, he said it with a more serious tone: "*Move your stuff into that office."* He said it in a comical yet serious way, as if he were saying, "Get your ass in there. Let's go."

We had two Finance and Insurance Managers. One was Corbett, who was Dennis's older brother, and the other was Randy Zucher. In the sales building, I had three Sales Managers, the two Finance and Insurance Managers, and typically about eighteen to twenty salespeople.

Tommy McDaniel was struggling with the fact that he had more experience in the sales operation than me, yet I was now the General Manager. I had much more experience in managing and leading people, but he had been in sales longer. When I would sit down and talk to Tommy about something, if any part of the conversation led to my making any suggestions about changing something in the Sales Department, I'd see an immediate change in the look on his face. He would remind me that he'd been in sales a long time and knew more about it than me.

One day when we were talking about some changes, he said, "Hey, Larry, I'm not going to do it. Look, I think you're going to do well in this job. I think you're going to learn a lot, but you don't know what you're doing now. I know what you're telling me is the wrong thing to do."

"Hey, Tommy," I said, "I don't think this is going to work."

"What do you mean?" he asked.

"I think you just need to go ahead and find a job somewhere else," I said.

He asked, "Are you firing me?"

"Yeah, that's exactly what I'm doing, Tommy."

"We'll see," he said, and he scooted back his chair. I watched him as he blew straight upstairs to Dennis's office.

I was thinking, *This could be the moment of reckoning.* It was new territory. Nothing this significant had occurred since I had taken my new position. I didn't know how Dennis was going to respond. Remember, now, he didn't like confrontations, and he fired people with handwritten notes. I knew this, so I just sat there, wondering what the outcome would be. Ten minutes passed, and then Tommy came downstairs, packed his stuff, and left.

Things began to change after that. Everyone saw that Dennis was in my corner. They also saw I wasn't going to put up with any BS. I wasn't out looking to terminate people, but I expected everyone to do their job and to work with me.

I found out early on that I rarely needed to terminate people. I just let them terminate themselves. I would tell them what the expectations were and ask them if they had the ability to do the job in line with those expectations. If they told me they needed some training or some help, I would get them whatever they needed. Now, if they didn't meet those expectations, we would need to talk about that person doing something else. It was that plain and simple. That's exactly how it was when I managed the little body shop in New Smyrna Beach, and it's exactly how I still operate my business today.

From a personnel perspective, the hardest thing a manager or a business owner does is to terminate someone. If anyone ever says they find joy in terminating someone, they have a problem. That's the toughest piece of my job.

I've seen managers terminate people in many cases when the firing was unjust because the manager had not made the person's responsibilities clear. If you hire someone without making the expectations clear, and then you terminate them because they didn't do the job properly, maybe their failure is your fault.

Leaders must be good communicators.

When Dennis moved me into the sales operation from my Service Director position, I had to hire a new Service Director. Myron Hammond had been the Service Director at a Toyota dealership about thirty miles from Daytona. He had an excellent reputation and had recently parted ways with his employer. After interviewing Myron twice, I hired him as the new Service Director for Sunrise Toyota Oldsmobile. Although I was in the training phase while Dennis was introducing me to the various sales positions, he asked me to supervise Myron because I was the most knowledgeable in the service business. Over time, it became obvious it wasn't going to work out with Myron.

Six months after being promoted to General Manager, I began my search for a new Service Director to replace Myron. One of the applicants was a guy by the name of Randy Johnson. He had limited experience. His father had owned a small, independent repair shop in West Virginia for much of Randy's life, and Randy had worked for him for years. Most recently, after moving to Florida, he had worked in a dealership as a Warranty Administrator. Although this is typically a service position, it is focused on only one piece of the business. Randy was one of the most enthusiastic, energetic people I had ever interviewed in my life.

During the first interview with him, I had expressed my concerns about his inexperience. I told him I liked his drive and determination, so I'd give it some thought. I knew I needed to make a change with Myron soon, but it wasn't the first thing on my list of priorities now that I was running the entire dealership and had a hundred employees. Needless to say, I was pretty busy.

I'd normally arrive at the dealership around 7:30 each morning after leaving the gym. A week after interviewing Randy the first time, I walked in as usual and said good morning to Maggie. She cut her eyes over to a person standing in the showroom. It was Randy Johnson. He was staring at me, smiling, and he gave me a goofy wave. I grabbed a cup of coffee and motioned for him to come back into my office. During this unscheduled, unofficial, second interview, Randy pleaded his case for the job.

I told Randy I liked everything about him except his lack of experience. I suggested he get a job as a Service Advisor in a dealership for a while to get some much-needed experience under his belt. He respectfully listened to my recommendation, but I could tell it wasn't what he wanted to hear. We wrapped up the interview, with both of us agreeing to give further thought to what we had discussed.

About two weeks later, I walked into the dealership one morning, and there was Randy Johnson, standing in the showroom once again. I invited him back to my office. After having a half-hour meeting, I offered him the Service Director position. I made it clear to him that I was hiring him strictly on his energy, enthusiasm, and determination. I figured that if he was willing to work as hard to keep the job as he did to get it, then he would be very successful.

Randy developed outstanding marketing skills for bringing new customers into the dealership. He immediately took our service business to a new level. He held the position for eight years and then simply outgrew us. He needed something bigger. He took a position as a corporate Service Director for a company that owned seventeen dealerships, and after a very successful career there, he opened his own national marketing company. He currently does business with hundreds of dealers nationwide, installing his service, marketing, and customer-retention programs. Randy and I remain very close today.

13

YOU HAVE TO SELL THE CAR FIRST!

Things were progressing nicely now. I had Randy managing the Service, Parts, and Collision Repair departments. My Sales and Finance Managers were settling in nicely, and the team was working well together.

Fortunately, due to my previous experience in various management positions, I had developed good leadership skills. I had been a department manager for several years now and had acquired a good reputation as a leader. I was probably more confident in my leadership skills than anything else. Now I had to focus primarily on strengthening my marketing skills.

The automobile dealership business is all about selling. You sell service in the Service Department and Collision Departments. You sell parts in the Parts Department. You sell extended service contracts, gap insurance, and prepaid maintenance contracts in the Finance and Insurance Department.

However, selling automobiles is the engine. If you don't first sell the vehicle, you can't sell any of the other services and products. It all starts with the sale of a vehicle. Salespeople and Sales Managers are compensated on how many vehicles they sell. The other managers have an opportunity to sell their products and services after a vehicle is sold. My responsibility as the General Manager was to provide my people *opportunities to sell*. When I did this, they followed me into battle. They did as I asked, and they had the utmost respect for me.

In the car business, we call this "having the ability to make something happen." All good leaders want to be known as someone who can make things happen.

Now that I had a solid team around me and I had developed good leadership skills, I simply had to become a great marketer so I could create opportunities for my team under any circumstances.

Other than doing the normal daily tasks required to run a successful auto dealership, I spent 100 percent of my time on marketing. I had a regular practice of arriving to work at 7:30 a.m. I would review reports, open mail, sign checks, walk through all the different departments to touch base with the department managers, and be back in the Sales Department by about 9:00 a.m. I would then return missed calls from the day before and get ready for my day.

After that, it was all sales. Nothing but selling cars and trucks. This was my primary responsibility, and I knew it.

I would make time for any marketing or advertising rep who walked into the dealership. I would read every journal, article, or book I could find on automobile marketing. I set out to become the best marketer in the business.

At the time, the Daytona/New Smyrna Beach area was primarily a retirement community. The biggest and best source for advertising automobiles was the newspaper. Boy, that has changed, but during those days, the newspaper was really popular and widely read.

However, I began to experiment with other marketing sources. I began doing a lot of direct mail, which became very popular. I also began writing newspaper ads that looked like newspaper articles—almost like a special-interest article about the dealership. These ads would be placed in the front section of the newspaper rather than in the classified section.

There is only a small percentage of newspaper readers who are in the market to buy a car or truck. If a reader was in the market, he or she would refer to the classified section, where retailers advertised their products. Most of the retailers who advertised there were automobile dealers. If a reader wasn't in the market to purchase a vehicle, the classified section usually went unread and into the trash. By running the ads in the front section of the paper, I hoped to catch the eye of someone who wasn't really in the market at that time. This worked well, as did my direct-mail campaigns. The more things like this I tried, the more traffic we had. The more traffic we had, the more vehicles we sold. The more vehicles we sold, the more parts, service, and extended service contracts we sold.

You *have* to sell the car first!

As we sold more vehicles, we had less turnover with our salespeople. Automobile sales has always had one of the highest rates of employee turnover of any business. As we were selling more vehicles and the word was getting out, more good salespeople from other dealerships would come apply for jobs. Selling vehicles cures all problems. It has never changed. It's still that way today.

The years 1986 and 1987 passed quickly. All was going well. By this time, Dennis had seen that I had things under control. He was happy with how we were performing. He was now having to spend less time with me because he clearly saw I was getting it done on my own. By this time, Dennis owned five dealerships. He was even beginning to share some of my marketing best practices with the guys running the other stores. That was a big compliment. We five General Managers were very competitive, so we didn't share successful sales promotions with each other. However, Dennis would. He had a vested interest.

I was learning more and more every day. By this time, I was frequently meeting with executives from Toyota and General Motors, as well as bankers and other professionals. It seems when you sell more cars, these guys come around more frequently. Most of these people were college-educated. I would pay close attention to their vocabulary. I would notice how good they were at listening and how they didn't interrupt when someone was speaking. I made mental notes of all this. When I was in a meeting with an executive, I always had a pen and pad handy for making notes. If I didn't know the definition of a word someone used, I'd jot it down on my note pad. When the meeting was over, I would look up the word to learn the meaning. I always kept a Webster's dictionary and a thesaurus in the top drawer of my desk. Boy, did I use them…

I would regularly receive business letters in the mail from automotive executives. We had no email back then. The letters were always perfectly written. The grammar and spelling were perfect. I would keep the letters in a file in one of my desk drawers. When I needed to compose a letter, I would use them as references. What's the old saying? "You've got to fake it until you can make it." That was me.

In addition to feeling better and having more confidence in my marketing and selling skills, I felt the same about my communication skills, especially when talking to highly educated people. In short order, my confidence was high, although I did not let it go to my head. I just felt comfortable in these meetings.

It was 1988 now, and I was thirty-two years old. I felt very comfortable in my position. I had grown a lot since that winter day two and a half years earlier, when Dennis put the note in the employees' boxes that said I had become the new General Manager of the dealership.

Susan, Linda, and me at our house on Patton Road in September 1959. I was three and a half years old.

Grandma and Grandpa Hill at their home in April 1960. This photo was taken shortly before his legs were amputated. I don't have memories of him before he lost his legs.

Dad and me in our yard on Patton Road,
December 1960.

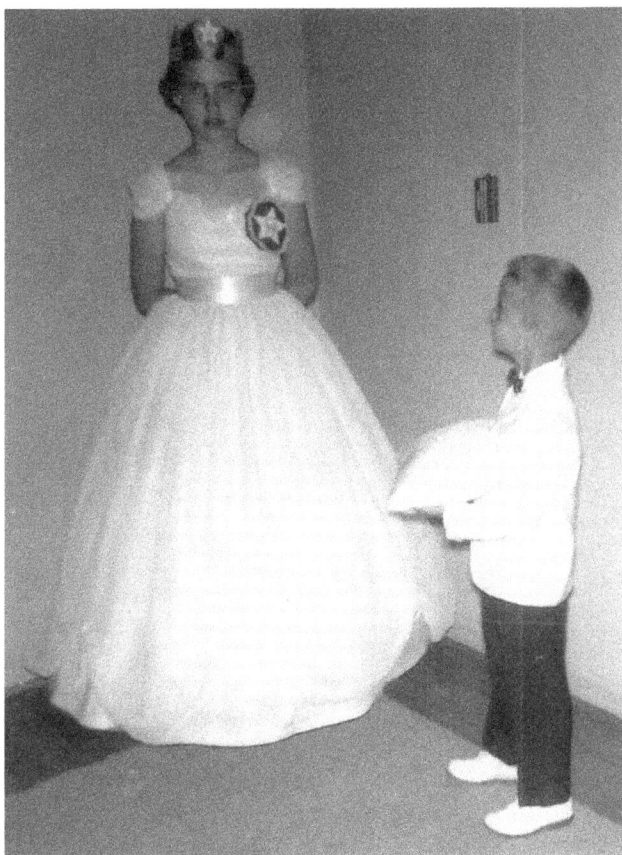

Linda and me before the Girls' Auxiliary banquet in
May 1961. I was the crown bearer.

Susan and me before attending the Girls' Auxiliary
banquet for Linda in May 1961.

Mom and Dad, Easter 1962.

Dad and me, ready for church, Easter 1965.

The Boylan-Pearce Department Store in Raleigh,
where my mom worked for a while in the late 1960s.

The paint and body shop I acquired from Ray
Rhinehart in 1977 in New Smyrna Beach.

Ponce de Leon Inlet, just north of New Smyrna Beach and just south of Daytona Beach. The red lighthouse is the tallest lighthouse in Florida.

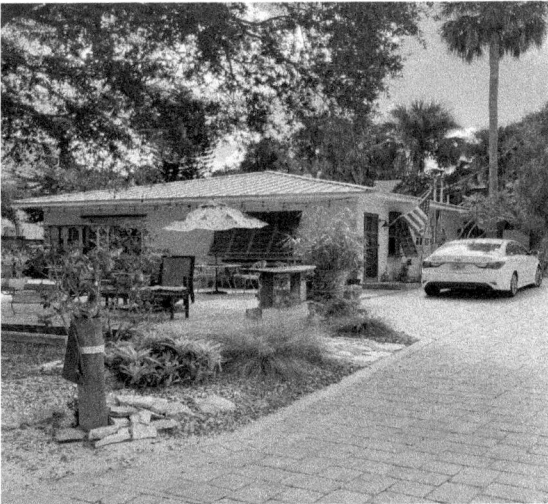

This is 107 Due East St., as it looked in the fall of 2023—the duplex in New Smyrna Beach, Florida, where I lived for many years.

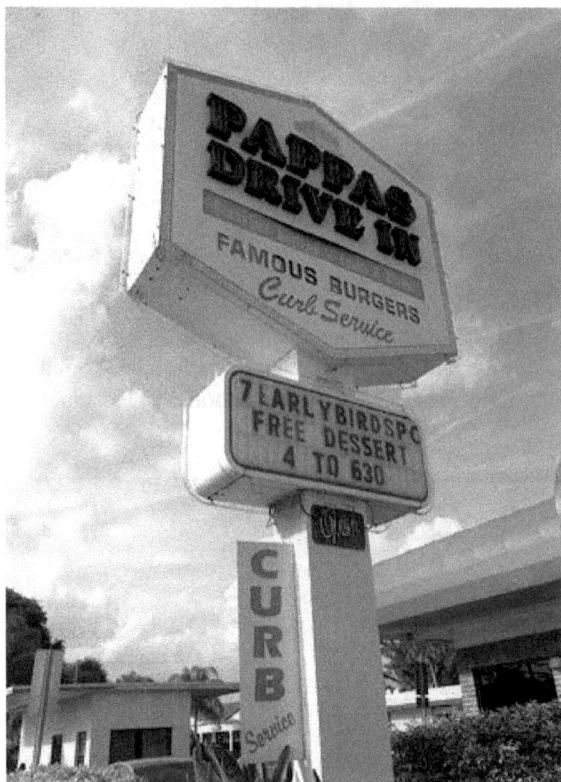

Pappa's Drive-In & Family Restaurant in New
Smyrna Beach, Florida.

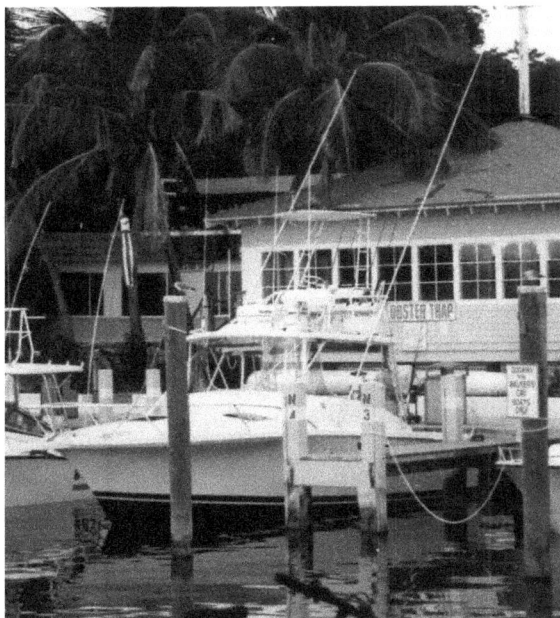

The fishing boat that Larry Williams and I owned at
Walker's Cay in the Bahamas.

Jim Newman, Larry Williams (my boat partner), and
me at the Daytona 500, in 1986 or 1987.

Me, on the left, catching my first sailfish in
December 1988 in Fort Lauderdale, Florida. The sea
was very rough; the others were inside the cabin,
taking turns getting sick.

My red 1973 Corvette, shown in 1983.

Dad holding one of our daughters; I think it's Emily.

Mom with Allison and Emily at our house in New
Smyrna Beach.

Mom with Allison and Emily on her pullout sofa in
her and Dad's condo in Raleigh.

Allison catches her first fish in Boone, North
Carolina.

Allison and Emily with our housekeeper, Norma, on a trip to the Dominican Republic. She slept all day when we were out; she may have had a night job as well.

Emily preparing to go on a ride with me. She would
wear only dresses during that stage of her life, and
that continued for about three years.

Allison and Emily before a surfing lesson in Hawaii.

Allison, Emily, and me in our hotel on a trip to
New York City.

Emily and Allison when we went on a father-daughter trip to New York City, maybe 2008.

Same NYC trip, with Emily and Allision in a FDNY truck.

Allison and Emily having their hair braided in the Bahamas. It doesn't look like they are having fun.

The family on a trip to the Bahamas.

Jill and me in front of St. Patrick's Cathedral in New York City, December 2009.

Jill and Annabel on a trip we took to the Bahamas.

Jill and me at a Breast Cancer Awareness fundraiser
in Chattanooga, Tennessee, probably 2010.

Jill and me at the Vatican in Rome, Musei Vaticani.

14

MY NEXT BIG OPPORTUNITY

Dennis and his cousin, Dick, who were partners at the Chevrolet Oldsmobile dealership, decided to part company. I didn't know the details, but the relationship soured and Dick left.

Dick's right-hand guy at the dealership was his Senior Sales Manager, Ron Desco. Ron had been with the dealership for many years and was a good sidekick. He had been there before Dick ever joined Dennis as his partner. Ron was a bit of a Nervous Nellie, a worrier of sorts. He liked working for Dick because Dick protected him. When Dick left, Dennis asked Ron to be the General Manager of the dealership. I think Dennis knew Ron wasn't General Manager material, but he felt he could do the job at least temporarily while he came up with a more permanent plan. Ron surely hated to see Dick leave, but I think even though he was nervous, he was happy about this opportunity to be the General Manager.

In addition to owning the Chevy Olds dealership in New Smyrna Beach, Dennis and Dick had purchased the Jeep dealership in town as well. The Jeep dealership was a small store that never really performed well. Very small dealerships are hard to operate. They require a lot of time to make a little profit. The Jeep store was struggling, and now the Chevrolet Oldsmobile dealership was also beginning to decline within a few months of Dennis making Ron Desco the General Manager. Dennis didn't put up with poor performance for very long, so I knew changes would be coming.

Dennis came up with an idea of how to fix the Chevy Olds store and the Jeep store. His intention was to share the plan with me as a "compliment." He said, "Hill, I have a plan. You have done a great job here. You have this place really humming and running on autopilot."

He had no idea he had just offended me. *The store did not run on autopilot.* I have always strived for my success to look effortless. I never wanted my boss or employees to see me stressed. When people see you stressed, they get scared. When they get scared, they start doubting your leadership. My goal was for my boss and staff to feel confident. I went into that dealership every day and put my shoulder into it. I made it appear effortless. It was not on autopilot—I was making it happen, which Dennis soon learned.

Dennis went on to say that he wanted me to move my office to the Chevrolet Oldsmobile dealership and fix both it and the Jeep store. Dennis owned the Ford dealership in New Smyrna as well, and he had a great guy named Bob running it. Bob was a quality guy and a quality operator. He still is to this day.

Dennis had hired a guy to run the Ford store and said he would move Bob to the Toyota Olds dealership to take my place. I was happy for this opportunity because it meant I could get out from under Dennis's shadow. Although I had progressed nicely at the dealership and was doing a good job, I was still under the same roof as Dennis each day. This was my opportunity to show him and the other General Managers that I could do it on my own.

I said, "OK, let's do it. What are we going to do with Desco?"

Dennis said he would let Ron know the plan and then move him back to Sales Manager. We planned to make the changes with Bob, the new Ford General Manager, Ron, and me in about two weeks. This would give Dennis time to inform everyone of the changes.

On September 1, 1988, I walked into the Chevy Olds store to take over. Ron was still in the General Manager's office. I visited with him for a few minutes and then finally said, "Ron, I'll need you to move back into the Sales Manager's office."

He looked puzzled and asked why.

I said, "Because I'm here to run the dealership. Didn't Dennis tell you?"

Here we go again, with Dennis being uncomfortable terminating people. Ron said Dennis had told him that I was coming to the dealership to help him with the Service and Parts Departments since I had a lot of experience in those areas of the business.

I said, "Ron, I have been running the largest dealership in the group for two years. Do you really think I'm here to run the Parts and Service Departments?" I reminded Ron that Dennis was not comfortable in this arena, and he just didn't want to hurt his feelings.

Ron moved back to the Sales Manager position. He wasn't happy, but he did it with a good heart. I served it up in a positive manner to the staff so he wouldn't be embarrassed. It worked out fine for the first month.

I put my belongings in the General Manager's office and then went directly to the sales desk. I needed to observe the sales process to get an understanding of why it wasn't working. I discovered the problem before lunchtime—there was no control over the sales process. Management was not in charge. The salespeople had free rein to do whatever they wanted, however they wanted. I went back to my office, closed the door, and made a plan. Then I went back to the sales desk and told the manager to let me have his seat. I sat there every day for the next 60 days.

During those two months, I would get to the dealership about 7:30, just as I had in Daytona. I would sign checks, open mail, meet with the other department managers, walk through the entire dealership, go down to the Jeep dealership and meet with the manager who ran the store, and be back on the sales desk before 11:00 a.m. I would run the sales desk until we closed that evening, go to my office to return phone calls, and do any other things I needed to do, and then finally go home. This was my daily routine for 60 days.

We stopped the bleeding at the Jeep dealership, and it began to make a modest profit. It was never going to make big money, but Dennis was happy because it was now at least profitable. My efforts did not make a huge difference, but I accepted the modest profit so I could focus on the Chevy Olds Store.

My big opportunity for profit growth was at the Chevy Olds store. Once I gained control of the sales process and implemented some of my proven best practices for maximizing sales and profit, we moved the needle significantly. We were selling cars and trucks and making good profits on them. Because the salespeople were compensated on sales and profits, they were happy. The managers were also happy because, although they were embarrassed by me showing them what a poor job they had been doing, they were also paid from sales and profit, so they experienced a nice pay increase.

Most importantly, Dennis was happy. I had shown him once again what I could do.

Ron Desco left after about a month, so I hired and trained a Sales Manager to take his place. The new guy I hired worked out well, so we just kept increasing sales and profit. All was good at both the Chevy Olds and Jeep stores.

After four or five months into my stint there, Dennis stopped by to see me one afternoon. He said, "I've got to tell you, I'm impressed with what you have done here, especially in such a short period of time. I guess you know we are struggling at the store in Daytona. I don't think it's a good fit for Bob."

Evidently, as rapidly as things were improving at the Chevy Olds and Jeep stores, business was quickly declining at the Toyota Olds dealership.

He didn't mention the "autopilot" thing again, but he sure knew that he had been incorrect in saying it the first time. This wasn't the case now. He said he wanted me to go back to the Toyota Oldsmobile store, and he would move Bob to the Chevy Olds store. The guy running the Jeep store was doing OK after we got a few things fixed.

Dennis is a smart guy. He always told me what he was going to pay me; we never discussed it. He never quite paid me what the job was worth because he knew he had taken a chance on me and offered me opportunities that many would not have. That's why I never complained, and I accepted whatever he said. However, this time was different. I had shown him I could get the job done. I told him what I wanted to be paid. I told him the salary I wanted and the percentage of the dealership profit I wanted. He agreed.

Now I was back at the Toyota Oldsmobile dealership, and Bob went to the Chevy Olds dealership. Shortly after Bob and I changed positions, we had lunch one day.

He said, "You know, Larry, it's not that I couldn't do the job at the Toyota Olds dealership. I just wasn't *willing* to do what it took to get the job done."

Bob and I were friends and still are today. We have been friends for almost forty years.

I really respected Bob for saying that. Truer words had never been spoken. Bob was a smart guy and a good car guy; it's just that all people aren't wired the same. I was at a point in my career where I wanted to see just how good I could become at running car dealerships, and I was going to do whatever I had to do and make the sacrifices to find out.

In all fairness to Bob, he was not prepared for what he stepped into with the General Manager position. Dennis had hired him after he was already in upper management. Bob, as most of the General Managers at Dennis's dealerships had, received previous training by someone other than Dennis. Running a dealership for Dennis, especially with his office being on-site, was new to Bob. Dennis was such a good operator and knew every aspect of the business so well, you could possibly feel like he was scrutinizing or "second-guessing" you.

Dennis had trained me, so I was accustomed to this. Being trained by him was like going to the auto-dealership version of Navy SEAL training, if there was such a thing. When I was at the Toyota Olds dealership and Dennis's office was there, I had one goal each day: to stay one step ahead of him. If I didn't, he would run over me.

It was all I'd ever known, but Bob wasn't familiar with this. It wasn't an easy dealership to run to begin with, but managing it and staying ahead of Dennis at the same time was probably overwhelming. Bob is a tough guy, and he never blamed his struggles on having to meander through Dennis's mine fields, but this surely added to them.

I settled back in at the Toyota Olds dealership. We were continuing to grow; however, things were beginning to change in the auto world. At one time, Oldsmobile had been one of the largest automobile manufacturers in the country. Now Toyota, the once little and unheard-of Japanese import, was making a ton of ground. Demand was growing year by year. Oldsmobile sales were dropping off drastically. The dynamics of the two brands were changing.

In the 1980s, we would sell 70 percent Oldsmobile and 30 percent Toyota. We were now at about 50–50, with Toyota getting a bigger percentage of our sales each year. Oldsmobile sales continued to drop off for the next decade. On April 29, 2004, the last Oldsmobile came off the assembly line, signaling the end of the 107-year-old brand. America's longest-surviving car company.

All was well at Sunrise Toyota Oldsmobile. We continued to grow every year. Sales were good, and Randy Johnson and his team were doing an outstanding job in parts, service, and the body shop. I enjoyed watching Randy grow in his position. The guy I hired based on nothing other than his energy had developed into the best Fixed Operations Manager I had ever known.

Our first daughter, Allison, was born on October 30, 1989, about three years after we moved into our new house. We were settling in nicely as a family of three.

15

DAYTONA AND NASCAR

When I ran the Toyota Oldsmobile dealership in the late 1980s and early '90s, Oldsmobile was very active in NASCAR racing. Buddy Baker, Sterling Marlin, and Harry Gant were three of the most popular Oldsmobile drivers.

When the Daytona 500, known as the "super bowl" of NASCAR racing, was held in Daytona every February, the town was packed with race fans. Oldsmobile Motor Company would send our dealership a new car for each of their drivers to use while they were in town for the race events. The Daytona 500 was always the first race of the year and the festivities surrounding the big race stretched out for two weeks.

As the Oldsmobile drivers would arrive in town, they would call me from the airport, and I would send someone over to pick them up with the car they would be using. I got to know Sterling Marlin some. He was a very nice guy and the closest to my age of the Oldsmobile drivers. Sterling was from Columbia, Tennessee, and was the son of legendary NASCAR driver Coo Coo Marlin. Sterling's sponsor was Piedmont Airlines at the time. Sterling would fly into Daytona on a Piedmont flight and call me from the airport.

Remember, there were no cell phones then. No text, no email. It was the days of old-fashioned pay-phone calling. Man, I miss those days…

Sterling had this soft Southern accent. He would call and say, "Hey, Larry, it's Sterling. I'm at the airport. Can you come get me?"

I would always go over myself and pick him up. He was just such a nice guy.

Back in those days, driving a green car was bad luck. I cannot remember how this superstition came about; however, Oldsmobile had sent a green car for Buddy Baker to use while he was in town.

He called me from the airport when the driver arrived in his green loaner car and said, "Larry, I'm not driving this green car."

I remember saying, "It's just to use on the street while you're in town. You aren't going to race it."

He said, "I don't care. I don't drive green cars."

I swapped it out for a car of another color.

Obviously, that superstition doesn't still exist because a lot of drivers have driven green cars for many years now.

I was always a big NASCAR fan, as were many, if not most, people from Daytona Beach. By the way, Daytona Beach was the home of NASCAR, and their headquarters is still there.

Although I pulled for the Oldsmobile drivers (until Oldsmobile got out of racing in 1991), I was always a big fan of Chevrolet driver Dale Earnhardt. Man, could he drive a race car. Dale Earnhardt was probably the best all-time racer ever. He sure was in my opinion, as well as the opinions of tens of thousands of others.

Dale drove most of his career for car owner Richard Childress. They were sure a winning team.

Dale was his own man and drove his own unique way. He always sat much lower in the race car than other drivers. He almost looked like a kid sitting behind the wheel. Word is that whenever his team built him a new race car, he would lower the seat himself. Even though back in his day, the restrictions and required specs for race cars and safety equipment were not as tightly controlled as today, many did exist. Therefore, when the seat manufacturer shipped a new seat, it had to be of a specific height, width, etc.

I have heard stories that Dale would personally don a welding helmet and gloves. He would fire up the old cutting torch, cut the seat frame down to the height he preferred, and weld it back together.

Dale never wore a full-face helmet or used the HANS device (head restraint). Both are mandatory in today's racing. The use of both, along with a plethora of other safety measures, were made mandatory since Dale's unfortunate death on February 18, 2001. He was involved in a final-lap collision in the 2001 Daytona 500. He crashed into a retaining wall after making contact with Sterling Marlin and Ken Schrader.

Dale had an outstanding career driving for Richard Childress. Retiring was probably on his radar for the near future, and he had started his own NASCAR team. The drivers for Dale Earnhardt Racing were his son, Dale Jr. (known throughout the racing world simply as Jr.) and racer Michael Waltrip, younger brother of Hall of Fame driver Darrell Waltrip.

Ironically, on the final lap of the 2001 Daytona 500, Michael Waltrip was leading, Jr. was in second, and Dale Sr. was in fourth. Who could have scripted this any better? Dale Sr. knew he could not get past Jr. and Michael to win. Racing is racing, and if Dale Earnhardt had to knock his mother out of the way to win, she was going into the wall. Plain and simple. That's how it's done.

Dale was going into turn four on the final lap, and his car got a little loose, causing him to hit the wall. I was there watching, and it did not appear to be a bad hit. I had seen many worse wrecks where the driver walked away unscathed. As he came off the wall, his number 3 Chevrolet made contact with Sterling Marlin and Ken Schrader. At this point, in a five-hundred-mile race, any of these contenders knew they had a chance at winning. Therefore, the six or seven drivers up front were racing as hard as they could.

Things happen awful quickly when you are traveling at 180 to 200 mph. I'm not sure anyone knows for sure exactly what happened in these final seconds, but there has been word that possibly Dale Sr. was attempting to block Sterling and Ken from getting to Jr. and Michael. Who knows?

Michael won the race, and Jr. finished second. It was Michael's first win racing for Dale Earnhardt Racing.

Unfortunately, Dale Sr. died of injuries he suffered in the crash. The racing world was in mourning.

That was the last NASCAR race I ever attended.

I have a picture hanging on the wall in my study of the winningest NASCAR driver of all time, King Richard Petty, racing in the 1984 Firecracker 400 in Daytona. The picture shows Petty alone on the back stretch of the speedway with Air Force One landing behind it at the Daytona International Airport. People ask me about the picture, and I tell them it is the perfect example of the old saying, "A picture is worth a thousand words." I'll explain.

Richard had earned the name "The King" because of his iconic racing career. Up until this race, he had won 199 NASCAR races. His nearest contender had won 105 (I'd say his record is safe). President Reagan was in office at the time and was flying to Daytona to attend a fundraiser dinner held that evening by no other than "The King" Richard Petty and the France family (the founders of NASCAR).

The *Daytona Beach News Journal* photographer got the perfect shot of Air Force One landing probably 40 feet off the ground with the number 43 Petty car directly below it. No other cars were on the back stretch. With forty-plus cars in a race, what are the chances of this? The runway for the airport sits just beyond the fence behind the back stretch of the speedway, so it appears as if Air Force One is landing on top of Petty's car. What a great picture.

President Reagan was on his way to Daytona when the race began. Air Force One was flying above South Carolina when Reagan made the announcement, "Gentlemen, start your engines" from the air. He landed when the race was about halfway over and was escorted to the France family suite above the speedway in plenty of time to see Richard Petty snag his 200th win. That would be King Richard's final NASCAR win.

About ten years ago, I was at a Ford function and met Mr. Petty. Although he had retired many years earlier as a competitive driver, he was still involved in the sport. His team had switched to Ford, so Ford Motor Company asked him to attend the event. He talked to me for about fifteen minutes, just one on one, as if he had known me his entire life. We did have a couple of connections. We were both originally from North Carolina, and I was living in the Daytona Beach area, where he spent a lot of time. Also, I was a Ford dealer, and he represented Ford on the racetrack.

I told him about my picture and the story. Ironically, he had never seen the picture. We were both surprised by this. As we finished up our conversation, I was walking away to give someone else the opportunity to talk to him. He quickly and politely excused himself from the next person for a minute and called out my name.

He said, "Hey, Larry" (I was surprised he remembered my name). I stopped and turned back. He said, "Thanks so much for telling me that story. It made my day."

He shook my hand again and walked back to the guy who was patiently waiting to talk to him. I could see the joy on his face. What a gentleman.

16

MOVING ON UP

Oddly enough, when much of the industry was struggling throughout 1991—the Persian Gulf War had Americans on edge, and the economy was unstable—we knocked it out of the park at the Toyota Oldsmobile dealership.

In late 1991, Bob decided to leave the Chevy Olds dealership and move to Dalton, Georgia. Dave Sale owned several dealerships throughout the Southeast area and had just bought a new dealership there. Dave offered Bob a partnership to move to Dalton and run the store. It was a good opportunity for Bob.

Ironically, Dave was the person who had originally put Dennis Higginbotham in business years earlier. When I had pulled up asking for a job in 1977 at the dealership in Florida with the name "Higginbotham" on the sign, I didn't know it then, but Dave Sale was the majority owner of the dealership. He was the person who had put Dennis in business.

I later learned that Dave and Dennis had hit it off when they met years earlier. Dennis had been hired by Chevrolet Motor Company after graduating from Auburn University. He was a dealer sales representative who traveled around his territory and called on Chevrolet dealers. Dave Sale was one of the Chevy dealers in Dennis's territory. Dennis and Dave became pretty close. One day he mentioned to Dave that he may like to become a Chevrolet dealer. Dave told Dennis that if he found a deal on a store that made sense, he would consider being his financial backer. Dennis began scrambling to find a dealership. He found the one in New Smyrna Beach. All Dennis had was some equity in his house and some money in his 401(k) retirement plan. David told him that he would invest 75 percent if Dennis could come up with the money to cover the other 25 percent.

I was a body-shop technician at the time and didn't know how these things worked. A couple of months after I began working, I saw a heavy-set, bald guy sitting in Dennis's office. I asked the receptionist who it was. She said, "That's Dennis's business partner, Dave Sale. He's the guy who got Dennis started into the dealership business." She went on to tell me about their arrangement. This marked the beginning of my education in ownership details.

I came to discover later that whenever Dennis and a business partner parted ways, it never ended amicably. After they were in a partnership for five years, Dennis bought Dave out, and it was an ugly, nasty end to a relationship. Dennis could no longer stand Dave Sale. Therefore, when Bob told

Dennis he was going to partner with Dave, Dennis hit the roof. He already despised Dave, and now he thought Dave was stealing one of his best General Managers. Dennis really liked Bob. It bothered him to see Bob leave. I could tell he was frustrated and upset.

During this time, Dennis was finishing a nice remodel on a bank building he had purchased in New Smyrna Beach. He was going to make it his office and would no longer have an office at the dealership. He informed me that he just didn't have the patience to manage the General Managers any longer. He wanted me to move into his current office upstairs at the Toyota Olds store and hire someone to take my place. I was to oversee all the dealerships and install in them the best practices I had employed in the past. Now all General Managers would report to me as Vice President of Higginbotham Management Company.

I had been with Dennis for many years now, and all the other General Managers knew me. They knew I had experienced quite a bit of success, especially during a time when most were struggling. They accepted me well as their new leader. I promoted one of my Sales Managers, Merle Simpson, to my position. I moved upstairs to Dennis's old office and began my new job. Dennis had a very good assistant in a small office next to his, and he left her there to work for me.

Dennis called one day while I was still in the process of turning the Toyota Olds responsibilities over to Merle and getting settled into my new position of overseeing all the dealerships. He said, "Pat Moran and Jim Press want us to meet with them next Monday afternoon at the Toyota headquarters in Deerfield Beach."

Pat Moran was the CEO of Southeast Toyota, which was founded by her father, Jim Moran. Jim Moran may be the best car guy to have ever walked the face of the Earth. He was an incredible visionary. Back in 1968, Toyota was just beginning to import cars to the United States. Toyota Motor Sales created distributorships across America to distribute the little-known Japanese economy vehicle. Jim Moran was a recently retired Ford dealer from Chicago who had just moved to South Florida. Mr. Moran had an incredible marketing reputation dating back to his Ford dealer days. He seemed exactly like what Toyota was looking for to represent their new product in the United States. Toyota asked Mr. Moran to be their southeastern US distributor.

I think the workaholic Moran got bored with retirement quickly after moving to South Florida, and he agreed to become the Toyota distributor. He founded Southeast Toyota Distributors in Deerfield Beach, Florida. Southeast Toyota sold new Toyotas to all Toyota dealers in Florida, Georgia, Alabama, South Carolina, and North Carolina. By the late 1980s, Mr. Moran, who was the chairman, promoted his daughter, who had worked in the business her entire life, to CEO. Jim Press, the president, was a high-integrity, very smart, and polished automobile executive.

Pat had called Dennis and asked him to come down to Deerfield the following Monday afternoon to share with her and Jim our secret for having such an outstanding sales year in 1991, when dealers were struggling nationwide. Dennis called me and said, "They are sending one of their planes to pick us up at 1:00 p.m. at the Daytona airport. They want to know how we had such a big year. I'll meet you at the FBO at the airport at 12:45." That's all he said. He didn't ask me to prepare a presentation or be prepared to tell them what we did. Just that he would see me at 12:45.

Dennis enjoyed the spotlight and wasn't crazy about sharing it. However, he knew he had no choice this time because he didn't know what I was doing to create all of the business.

Jim Press and Pat Moran didn't even know who Larry Hill was. At their level, they talk only to the dealership owner. The Toyota representative I dealt with on the dealership level was a guy named Chris Verner. He was the one from Southeast Toyota who would come to the dealership each month. Chris would meet with me when he came to the dealership. He rarely even saw Dennis. Chris knew about the successful marketing campaigns I had used in 1991 to create the record sales. He would come in and ask what I was doing, and I'd show him. He'd high-five me, take me to play golf, and buy beer afterward. He loved it. I'm sure he had mentioned me to Pat and Jim; however, they still dealt only with dealership owners.

I had a four-day notice from the day Dennis called until the Monday we were going to meet with them. I prepared a presentation with personalized copies for everyone who would be in the meeting. I met Dennis at the airport on Monday. We both wore business suits, which was my common daily work attire in those days. The plane was there, and we took off at 1:00 p.m. for the short flight to Deerfield

Beach. Once we were in the air, I opened my briefcase and handed Dennis his copy of the presentation.

I said, "I brought this in the event you wanted to review it with them."

Dennis had just begun wearing reader glasses and hated them as much as we all do. He held the presentation away from his face and squinted a little. Handing it back to me he said, "You handle the presentation."

Chris Verner was there to greet us when we landed. We engaged in small talk during the fifteen-minute drive to the Toyota headquarters.

We arrived and went into a conference room where Pat and Jim were waiting. Naturally, they knew Dennis. Chris introduced me and said a few nice words. Jim turned to Dennis and me and said, "Gentlemen, we asked you to come down here today to find out how you sold so many new Toyotas in a year when most of our dealers struggled, and some mightily." He went on to say, "I want to bottle your secret and take it to our other 160 Southeast dealers."

I took this as the highest compliment I had ever been paid to date. Maybe of all time.

After we talked for a few minutes, Dennis said, "Hill, share the material we brought with these folks." Ha! The material "we" brought. I went through the presentation for about twenty minutes, and we talked for about another twenty or so minutes. Then Chris took us back the airport, where the pilots were waiting to take us back to Daytona. That was a good day.

Shortly thereafter, Dennis and Anne's first of two children, Trudy, graduated from the University of North

Carolina in Chapel Hill. Trudy was a very smart young lady. I had known her since she was a kid, working in some of the various departments in the summers while in high school. She was wired much like her dad.

Dennis walked into my office one morning along with Trudy and said, "Here she is, Hill. Turn her into a car guy."

I put together a training plan to get her going. She was a wonderful student. She accepted every assignment I gave her with a great attitude and always performed well. It reminded me a little of Dennis training me. It was fun working with someone who really had a strong desire to be a successful auto dealer. Trudy worked hard in various positions and was doing well.

A couple years into her "on-the-job" training, Dennis purchased the Mercedes dealership in Daytona Beach. The facility was old and really beaten up. It was by no means what you would have expected of a Mercedes dealership. Mercedes told Dennis he had twelve months to move it to a facility they would approve. I suggested he talk to Steve Lucas, the owner of the Acura dealership in Daytona. Steve was a successful Honda dealer in Jacksonville, Florida, and Honda (the parent company of Acura), had awarded him an open Acura point in Daytona about ten years before. He built a new Acura facility next door to the BMW dealership. Steve really struggled with Acura. The Daytona market was just not big enough for a single-point Acura dealership. We didn't even have a Lexus store in Daytona because Lexus didn't feel it was a big enough luxury market. Acura was and had been a low-volume car company.

I told Dennis I was sure that Steve Lucas would probably consider selling the Acura store. Dennis called me from his office a couple days later and said, "We are having lunch with Steve Lucas Monday. He's going to drive down from the Honda store in Jacksonville and meet us at Acura. I'll pick you up at 11:30."

Dennis picked me up at the Toyota store, and as we drove to the Acura dealership, he updated me on the conversation he'd had with Steve a few days earlier. Steve had agreed to sell the dealership and had given him a price. I can't remember the exact price, but I do remember that it was very low—especially for us because we had a need. I couldn't believe it when Dennis told me. The price Steve had given him was probably less than the real estate value. It was super-crazy low.

I jokingly said to Dennis, "Why are we meeting him, to bring a check?"

Neither of us had ever met Steve. He and Dennis had heard of each other but had never formally met, and he had no idea who I was. We pulled up in front of the Acura dealership, and Steve walked out. I hopped in the back seat, and Steve sat up front with Dennis. We drove another five minutes to Indigo Golf Club and had lunch. We made small talk for a while, and then Dennis confirmed with Steve that the price he had been given on the phone included everything—real estate, parts, other assets, etc. Steve assured him it did. The dealership was ten years old. It was in good condition and just needed a little TLC to meet the Mercedes luxury facility requirements. Bang—a no-brainer.

After lunch, when we were dropping Steve off, Dennis said, "Steve, I'll pay you this amount for the dealership." I can't remember the number, but it was about $200,000 less than what Steve had said he would accept. The $200,000 was peanuts in the whole scheme of things, but sometimes business guys, especially car guys, think they must negotiate everything. You have to know when and when not to ask. Some people struggle with this.

Steve got very angry. He said, "Dennis, I told you last week on the phone what my bottom number was and that I would not accept a penny less. Now, I've driven all the way down here from Jacksonville just to hear this bullshit."

He got out of the car and stormed into the dealership. Dennis pulled out and drove back to the Toyota Olds dealership. I was still in the back seat. Ha! He didn't say a word. It was total silence as he drove. When we returned to the Toyota dealership, he pulled up to the front, put the car in park, and said, "What do we do now?"

Ha! "What do *we* do now?"

I said, "You call him back. You tell him that you are stupid. You say, 'Look, Steve, I'm an idiot. You're right—you told me what you wanted and that you wouldn't take a penny less. My mistake. Sometimes as a car dealer, I just think I need to negotiate everything. I apologize for offending you. I'll accept your deal.'"

By the way, I agree with Dennis that we do need to consider negotiating every deal. However, sometimes we just have to read people and the situation and leave egos out of it. Although neither of us had met Steve Lucas before, I had heard over the years that he was a bit of a loose cannon, that he was known to blow up quickly. Well, the stories were correct.

Apparently, Dennis took my advice about calling Steve, apologizing, and agreeing to the original number because we closed on the Acura dealership. A few months later, we moved Mercedes into the facility. Trudy had really progressed nicely, and we made her General Manager of the Mercedes store. We surrounded her with some of our best people who were a good fit for a luxury store, and we were set to go. We sent Tom Pelchen over as her New Vehicle Manager, Steve Rollins as her Used Vehicle Manager, and longtime great employee Bruce Jones as the Service Manager. All three of these guys were longtime employees at some of the other dealerships we had and were all true professionals.

We opened the dealership with a solid team, and the store took off quickly.

We made some renovations to the old, worn-down original Mercedes facility and turned it into a big used-car operation called Sunrise Auto World. It was in a part of town with a lot of blue-collar traffic on a major four-lane road. I took one of our outstanding used-car salesmen who had been with us a while, Don Clark, and made him the manager. Within a year, we were selling over one hundred used cars a month from that facility.

In the meantime, Dennis sold the low-profit Jeep dealership to the local Dodge dealer. We opened our own finance company named HMC Finance for people with lower credit scores who typically bought used cars.

Our group of dealerships was now Sunrise Toyota Oldsmobile, Sunrise Auto World, Higginbotham Mercedes,

Higginbotham Chevrolet Oldsmobile, Halifax Ford, and HMC Finance Company. All the businesses were in Volusia County, within twenty-five miles of each other.

We had everything in one nice location down the coast in Volusia County. We had good General Managers in all the dealerships. I focused heavily on marketing and installing many of the best practices in the other stores that I had established in the Toyota Olds store. The businesses were doing well.

Things didn't seem to stay the same for long in Dennis's world, as you can probably tell from the book so far. Change is good. It keeps everyone young and growing. Dennis could get bored easily and always wanted a new project. He seemed to be happiest and most content when he had a new project. Now, with my current position as vice president of his company, many of his new projects involved me.

17

BUSINESS-TRIP
ADVENTURES

My second daughter, Emily, arrived on May 25, 1993. Gayle was a stay-at-home mom, taking great care of our girls. I was doing my thing, managing the car dealerships.

During this time, we hired a gentleman named Bill Lint. He was a retired Exxon Oil executive and was a little bit of an odd bird. He had been married at one time, and he and his wife were divorced in 1956, the year I was born. This gives you an idea of how long he had been divorced and on his own. Bill wanted something to do. He loved talking to people and being around people, so we hired him as a runner.

A runner must be a very responsible person. Their job is to take the deposits to the bank a couple of times a day, go to the title offices to drop off the paperwork for recently purchased autos, hand-deliver specific documents the dealer or General Manager needs to send to other businesspeople, occasionally go to the airport to pick up executives who might be coming to the dealership, etc. Much of their work is behind-the-scenes, but it's a very important job.

Bill loved his job as a runner. He loved being there to help us out, and he loved going to the bank every day. He knew all the young women who worked there and was a bit of a ladies' man, but he was harmless. He was in his late sixties but wouldn't talk to a woman if she was over thirty-five years old! He liked the young ladies. Ha! That's just how he was.

Bill was also a pilot. He owned a nice single-engine, four-place plane. It was a fast, sleek, low-wing plane with retractable gear.

I frequently had to go to Miami for Toyota business meetings. Despite the short distance from our dealership, it wasn't a quick trip if you were flying commercial. The flight from Daytona to Miami would first take you north to Atlanta, then back south over Daytona, and then on to Miami. When I had to make these trips, I'd get Bill Lint to take me in his airplane. When we would go to meetings, Bill would wear a business suit, just as I did, and he would attend the meetings with me. I assume others thought he was a dealership manager, but they were probably somewhat confused because he usually slept through the meetings! This was fine with me. I wanted a well-rested pilot taking me home.

It was interesting flying with Lint. He was a nice guy and a good pilot, and we enjoyed talking during our flights.

One weekend, I was going fishing with some guys in Marathon, Florida. I wanted to get Bill to fly me down there. I said, "Friday afternoon, I'd like you to fly me down to Marathon, drop me off, then take the twenty-minute flight farther south to Key West. It's a fun place to hang out for a couple of days. I'll cover your hotel room for two nights. Come back to Marathon on Sunday, and we'll fly back to Daytona." Bill said he would be happy to do this.

Bill would have been fine making the trip by himself because he loved people and never met a stranger. However, I thought he'd have more fun if our mutual friend, Wayne, went with him. I felt bad about asking him to spend the weekend by himself.

I told Wayne that I wanted him to go with us. I said, "Wayne, I want you to go down to Key West with Bill and hang out with him for the weekend so he's not doing it by himself. I will pay for a room for you and him. Wayne agreed and was looking forward to it.

We met at the airport across from the dealership on Friday afternoon, got in Bill's plane, and took off toward Marathon for the first leg of the trip. Wayne was in the back seat and fell asleep shortly after takeoff. I was sitting up front, talking with Bill.

We had been handed off to the Miami control tower and were entering heavy air traffic. Bill and I were both wearing headsets and could hear the air traffic controllers talking. Out of nowhere, all the electronics in the plane stopped working. Our headsets went silent, the gauges on the control panel dropped down to zero, and the lights went dark. The only thing still working was the spinning propeller outside the front windshield. Thank God it was still turning. I never took my eyes off the propeller.

Bill was a smart guy and a good pilot. He tried a couple of things, but nothing seemed to work. He said to me, "We have to get out of this Miami traffic quickly. We can't be here in this congested airspace without any communication." He immediately banked the plane to the left and headed east.

As we headed east, I began to see the Atlantic Ocean. Fortunately, all up and down the coast of Florida there are active airports that had originally been used by the military in World War II. Bill handed me a thick binder with laminated pages. On each page there was information about a specific airport, including a drawing of the runway configuration and a list of the services and amenities they offered.

As Bill flew us over the airports, I would look down at the runway, then quickly look up and flip through the pages, trying to recognize it. Finally, I matched a runway configuration to a page. "That's Pompano Airport," I said. "And it has rental cars and mechanics. Bill, we can land there."

We started heading toward the airport and made a circle around it. Bill said, "See the big white cannon-looking thing on top of the tower? Tell me when it flashes a green light."

When pilots fly over an airport during an emergency and cannot communicate with traffic control, they will circle the airport at a low altitude. When the control tower sees this, they know the pilot is sending a signal, asking for permission to land. Once it's safe for the plane to land, they flash a green light out of this big cannon. The second time we made the low loop around the airport, the green light flashed, indicating it was safe to land.

Wayne woke up while we were taxiing the plane up to the airport. By this time, it was about 5:20 p.m. All the mechanics had left for the day, so we rented a car and drove the rest of the way to Marathon. They dropped me off and went to Key West.

I was very thankful to be able to fish with my friends. On Sunday, Bill and Wayne returned with the rental car. We drove it back to New Smyrna, and a few days later, after the plane was repaired, Bill drove back down to pick up his plane and flew it back home.

I spent a lot of time flying all around the southeast with Bill Lint, but this was the most adventurous trip we ever had.

Dennis always had planes as well. He began with two or three different King Airs and then moved up to jets. Dennis would frequently offer his jet and pilots to me for business trips.

A couple of days after I would return, I would receive an invoice from him for the pilot and the hours spent on the plane. At the time, this was around $3,000 per hour. I personally didn't have to pay this; it was for me to split among the dealerships. However, I was paid a percentage of the dealership's profits, so this expense did affect me somewhat personally.

I usually just kept quiet about my scheduled business trips and would fly commercial. I could get a very nice first-class seat for much less than it cost to use his plane.

It did make sense for me to use his plane if I was taking some of the management team with me. There was a meeting in St. Louis one December in which I needed to take the service managers from all the dealerships. Since there were six of us, using Dennis's plane was more economical than buying six commercial tickets.

We arrived late on Friday to prepare for an all-day meeting on Saturday at our hotel near the airport. Around midday Saturday, it began to snow really hard. It snowed all afternoon. As my guys and I enjoyed dinner later that evening at a nice restaurant in downtown St. Louis, I noticed the snow was still falling heavily. We finished dinner and went back to the hotel. We were scheduled to meet the pilots at the airport the following morning at 8:00.

When we arrived, I noticed the door was open and the stairs were down on the plane. The pilot and his copilot were sitting in the cockpit of the plane going through their preflight routine. Since the door had been left open, it was freezing cold.

After a few minutes of sitting in there shivering, I asked the pilot, Calvin, "Do you think we might be able to close the door?"

He said, "I will as soon as I can. We are going in and out of it right now as we study the manual to figure out how to de-ice the plane."

I quickly said, "Hey, man. Take your time. No hurry. Be sure you know how to use the deicers."

Everyone got a big laugh about this.

We made it home safely and had an uneventful trip. Also, I enjoyed the reminder of how quickly people can change their environment. We were sitting on the tarmac in below-freezing weather, and then three hours later, I was standing on the first tee at the Sugar Mill Country Club in New Smyrna in a short-sleeve golf shirt and no jacket, getting ready to tee off in the Florida sunshine.

On another occasion, I used Dennis's plane to take some of our management team to a required five-day training seminar in Michigan. The group was composed of my Service Director, Randy Johnson; longtime salesperson, T. L. Kays; Sales Manager, Tom Pelchen; salesperson, Gary LaFond; and General Manager, Elton Wetteland. The seminar was held at a General Motors training center in a very remote area about fifteen miles from downtown Detroit.

Our small chain hotel, maybe a Hampton Inn, was on the interstate about five miles from the training center. A bus would pick us up at 7:00 a.m. and bring us back at 7:00 p.m. These were long, intense days.

We ate all three of our meals each day at the training center. The food reminded me of middle-school cafeteria food—it was awful. One day, we finished early, around 5:00, and were driven back to the hotel. We were on our own for dinner for the first time since arriving.

The hotel was booked to capacity with dealership employees from around the country who were also attending this seminar. There was only one small café in the hotel, and it only held thirty or so people. The food there was as bad as the training center. My guys and I were desperate for a nice, gourmet meal and some good wine.

We gathered outside in front of the hotel. I could see across the interstate what looked like a restaurant. I asked the concierge about it, and he said it was a very nice Italian restaurant. I immediately asked if they had transportation.

Although I could see the restaurant from where we were, it wouldn't be possible for us to walk there. It was beyond the interstate and off a couple of interchanges and exit ramps, and there was also a huge embankment to cross. Besides, I had no interest in crossing traffic on foot over the interstate.

The concierge suggested we call a cab. We waited for over an hour for it to arrive—it most likely had to come all the way from Detroit—but when it eventually did, we were thankful to be headed to the restaurant!

We had wonderful Italian cuisine, drank wonderful Italian red wine, and just had a great time. Around 10:00, as the restaurant was preparing to close, we realized we had not thought to call for a return cab. After calling different companies, I soon found out there were no cabs available this late in this remote area. We were stranded.

Walking outside, we could see our hotel, but we faced the same challenges we had earlier: the traffic, exit ramps, terrain, etc. Only now it was even worse because of the darkness.

I made the executive decision that we were going to walk back to the hotel. It was our only option.

We started out by climbing over a couple of fences that separated the roadways from the privately owned properties. Then we navigated the wet, slippery embankments as we scuttled down toward the interstate. It began to appear we were home free until we realized the embankment that we were about to descend ran into a wide water-retention ditch. With limited vision due to the darkness, we estimated this drainage ditch was probably four to five feet wide. We knew we had to gather as much speed as possible going down the embankment so we could jump over this ditch.

Gary LaFond and I were the tallest in the group, both over six feet. To make sure no one got stranded, I decided we would send the shortest guys first. The shortest was Tom Pelchen, who was very athletic. He barreled down the embankment and successfully cleared the ditch.

I accepted the role as the captain of the ship and decided to be the last one to make the plunge. The first four guys successfully cleared the ditch while Gary and I remaining at the top. Gary looked at me and said, "Boss, you go. I'll be right behind you."

I took off and, as did my predecessors, cleared the ditch. We were all then standing on the hotel side of the ditch waiting for Gary. He started running down that embankment and made a beautiful, high leap. He was going to easily clear the ditch. Suddenly, when he was in midair, his body appeared to stop moving forward. He was at the height of his jump, but somehow his entire body froze. He dropped straight down and slowly sank up to his waist in the muck of the ditch.

We were shocked. (The first thing that came to mind was to roll in laughter. We resisted, though, because it was cold, and all we could see was the top half of Gary, and he wasn't saying anything). We also didn't know if he was hurt.

We quickly decided to form a human chain, and I was going to reach down and give him a hand out of the ditch. Fortunately, it worked. Gary came out of the ditch unscathed, but he was coated in a thick layer of muck from his waist down and missing one shoe.

Gary said, "I've got to get my shoe."

I said, "It's impossible. Your shoe is gone. It's at the bottom of that ditch. You're going to just have to go with one shoe. Let's go."

We successfully crossed the last four lanes of the interstate and arrived at the hotel. Because of the overcrowded condition, the lobby was packed. We walked through the hotel with Gary in tow, squishing as he walked on one shoe and covered in black muck, as if everything was perfectly normal.

Later, Gary told us the muck was so thick on him that he couldn't get his pants off before getting in the shower. He threw the pants away afterward. Thankfully, he happened to have brought a second pair of shoes for the trip.

18

A NEW CHEVROLET OLDS DEALERSHIP

Dennis's very first dealership was the little Chevrolet Oldsmobile store where I had started working for him in 1977. Although we had added on to the building a couple times and had done a lot of renovations, it was beginning to show its age. This was Dennis's baby—his first—and he was proud of it.

He decided it was time to build a new facility and began working with a local architect to design a massive state-of-the-art dealership. While he was working on this new project, we were all just going to work every day, doing what we did. My days were packed with reviewing the performance of each store and helping the General Managers with problems or projects. I communicated with all the General Managers daily and often spent time with them in their dealerships.

Dennis decided he wanted to build the new dealership on the same piece of property it was on currently. This can be tough. It means you have to continue operating the business on a construction site, basically. They would tear off a piece of the old building to make room for a piece of the new building. The employees had to cram into a smaller area. We even had to rent some portable office trailers for additional office space. It was very cumbersome and exhausting. It took the contractors nine months to a year longer than expected to build the new facility because they had to work around everyone. It was a slow process. It's hard enough to keep salespeople when they are working in ideal conditions. This was even tougher.

My suggestion was to go out to Highway 44 (which is now "automobile row" in New Smyrna Beach), purchase a ten-to-twelve-acre parcel there, which was still reasonably priced at the time, and just build a new facility. We wouldn't miss a beat at the old location, and then we could just move into the new facility. We would not miss one day of business. But Dennis felt attached to the current location. He had some sentimental ties to it. That old location by now was more desirable for something other than a car dealership, so selling the old property for a good price would have been easy. But that's not what Dennis wanted to do, so we got started on the new facility at the current site.

As the project began to get underway, I could tell that Dennis wished I was there on-site. However, my office was at the Toyota Olds dealership in Daytona Beach, about thirty minutes away.

I'm not sure of all the details, but Dennis never really cared for Toyota or the Toyota people. He was a domestic car guy. He had worked for General Motors after he graduated from Auburn University. Then he owned a Chevrolet dealership, an Oldsmobile dealership, and a Ford dealership. He had also owned a Buick GMC dealership and a Toyota dealership. Although Toyota had the best long-term profit potential, he just didn't like it. I came to learn that Toyota felt the same way about him. He wasn't their favorite guy—maybe because he owned so many domestic stores. They like their Toyota dealers to live, eat, and sleep Toyota.

During the initial phase of the new Chevrolet Oldsmobile project, Dennis began having some conversations with Toyota about selling the dealership. He wanted to accomplish two things: 1) disassociate himself from Toyota, and 2) get me in New Smyrna during this construction project.

Within six months, he had accomplished both. Dennis sold the Toyota Olds dealership to the Harley Davidson dealer in Daytona, who had previously been a Toyota dealer. I moved my office to the "construction site" in New Smyrna. Because there wasn't room for two managers, I sent the current manager to another one of our dealerships.

Now my plate was completely full. I was running the dealership during the eighteen months of construction, while also handling my other responsibilities at the other dealerships. The employees were constantly complaining about the working conditions, and it was difficult to keep them focused on productivity.

Although it was a huge headache, and there was nothing easy about it, we ended up doing well. I overheard

Dennis tell a dealer friend that if the dealership just broke even during the construction, he would be happy. We actually maintained the same level of profitability during the construction that we had for the previous several years. We were all a little surprised.

Over the years, Dennis had allowed me to buy ownership in the Toyota Olds store. When we sold it, he wanted me to trade my ownership for part of the new Chevy Olds dealership. I agreed but was not excited about it because of my concerns over its profit potential due to the huge overhead expenses. We were building a huge, modern, state-of-the-art dealership. Something one might see in South Florida, such as Palm Beach or Miami. It had a multilevel parking deck, a two-story building, elevators, etc., and was very expensive.

Dennis had hired a local architect to design the building. Unfortunately for us, he was a high-end residential architect. Typically, architectural firms that specialize in designing dealerships are hired for such projects. There are many unique, specific pieces that go into the design. This guy, having little or no experience in this area, just didn't know about these details.

A perfect example was that he designed it with a solid front facing the parking lot. There were no windows. When the front of the building is solid, the salespeople cannot see when a customer arrives. Dennis was a sharp car guy. I was surprised he let that big piece slip by him. Also, the building was so big and had such a huge footprint on the property that we couldn't stock any more vehicles than we could before the renovation. It really looked more like a big, modern office complex than a car dealership. Big building and little parking. A car dealership should be just the opposite. In addition, the cost was astronomical. I was well aware of the cost and knew it was too high for a car dealership in a market of less than forty thousand people.

I could tell Dennis was getting concerned about the size and expense. One day he even dropped his guard and said, "Hill, I think I screwed up." Something he rarely said.

"Hey man, don't worry," I told him. "It's going to be beautiful. We'll make it work."

All the time, I was wondering *how*?

19

OUTSIDE FAMILY AND WORK

There are two hobbies I've always enjoyed: golf and offshore fishing. Unfortunately, in my profession, I had little time for either before retirement but enjoyed both.

Larry Williams, a really good friend of mine, and I owned an offshore fishing boat. He was the most generous and happy-go-lucky person you could ever meet. He was an avid hunter and fisherman. Williams never let anything get him stressed. I worried that he might die one day of a heart attack or something from having never walked into a gym, and for his desire to eat only fried foods, but I knew he would never die from stress.

Larry and his wife, Judy, had two children, Terry and John. They were a great family. The only times I had gone deer or quail hunting, Larry had taken me. While I had already fished offshore many times before meeting him, he taught me a lot. Our boat was a thirty-two-foot offshore boat with a flybridge and a stand-up cabin that slept four people. It had a galley, a shower and head, and heating and air conditioning. It was a nice, comfortable offshore boat.

Williams knew a young guy named Bob who was about thirty years old. Bob was a great fisherman. Williams and I decided we were going to take the boat for five days to a place in the Bahamas named Walker's Cay. We took Bob with us to be the mate because he knew all about how to rig the tackle and do minor maintenance on the boat.

Walker's Cay is a small fishing island at the northwest end of the Bahamas, a part of the North Abaco district. It's very rustic. Its nicest feature is a beautiful marina with a large, air-conditioned "fish cleaning" room. This was a luxury. When you came in with your catch at the end of the day you didn't have to stay out on the hot dock cleaning your fish. There was also a nice, clean hotel. It wasn't luxurious, but it was clean and had cold air as well. The hotel also had one of the best restaurants you've ever eaten at in your life. The people at Walker's Cay knew exactly what fishermen wanted: a great dock and marina, a clean hotel with air conditioning, and great food.

We left New Smyrna Beach one morning and took the boat down the Intracoastal Waterway to Stuart, Florida. That was a full-day run because you can only go so fast due to the many no-wake zones in the Intracoastal. We stopped at a marina at the inlet that leads out to the ocean in Stuart and docked the boat there. It was a nice resort to spend the night before we made the four-hour run to Walker's in the morning. Williams and I got a room, and Bob stayed on the boat. It had everything he needed, and he was happy.

The next morning, Williams and I got up about 6:00 and went down to the boat to greet Bob and prepare to leave. We quickly realized none of the electronic devices were working. No one knew what could have possibly happened. They had been working perfectly the day before when we docked.

There we were, about to cross the Gulf Stream in the Atlanta Ocean and head to a tiny island that was already like a needle in a haystack, and we had no navigation, GPS, radio, or radar. We had nothing.

Williams had been to Walker's Cay many times, probably fifteen or twenty times before now, and he was a fearless man. He had the most positive outlook of any person I'd ever known. After about an hour of messing around with the electronics, I came to the realization we were probably going to have to cancel or at least postpone our trip. Then Williams said, "Untie the boat. Come on, we're going."

So we left without our instruments. Naturally, I didn't feel comfortable about this, but I had to think we would be OK because Williams seemed so confident. He wouldn't have suggested we go if he didn't feel good about it. At least this is what I thought at the time. We pulled out of the inlet at Stuart and headed to the Bahamas with nothing but a compass. Williams was a smart guy, knew the boat and ocean well, and had no fear. Thirty minutes later, land was no longer in sight. We were out in the Atlantic Ocean, crossing the Gulf Stream with no electronics. Not even a two-way radio to use in the event of an emergency.

As we crossed, the current was continuing to push our boat north. Captains love to get in the Gulf Stream if they're headed north. It pushes them faster. But we were headed east. Had our electronics been working, they would have been constantly recalculating to tell us how much to steer the boat south to offset the northern current.

We'd been running for about two hours when Bob, the mate, started getting some tackle and supplies together. Williams was up top, running the boat from the flybridge, and I was below him on the main level. At about the same time, Williams and I both noticed a boat on the horizon headed our way. It was moving in our direction quickly. As it approached, we waved for them to stop. (How ironic that we were out in the middle of the ocean with the chances of seeing another boat almost nonexistent. Yet there we were, incredibly close to this boat). It was unreal.

The boat was a thirty-foot Contender center console fishing boat with three guys. It was a very fast offshore boat, built for speed. The trip that would have normally taken us four hours would have taken them about two hours.

When they idled up next to us, we asked if they had been to Walker's. They said they had. We asked them how their fishing trip had gone, and they told us it had been very successful. Williams told them we didn't have any electronics, only a compass, and asked them if they could give us a heading to Memory Rock.

Memory Rock is a vast rock formation that sticks out of the water from the ocean floor. It's located a few miles outside Walker's Cay. When you're right on top of it, it seems big, but out there in the middle of the Atlantic Ocean, you could miss it and never see it. It's like a grain of salt floating out there.

One of the guys gave Williams the coordinates to Memory Rock, and also the final setting from there on to Walker's Cay.

We said farewell to them and ran for another hour or so. All of a sudden, Williams shouted, "Land ho!" This is what pirates supposedly shout when they see land. We idled up to Memory Rock. From there we took the compass setting the guy had given us and headed toward Walker's.

Larry said to Bob and me, "OK, gentlemen. We cheated death again. How about pouring the captain a Scotch?"

I got out his Scotch, poured some in a red Solo cup, and added some ice. As I was taking it to him, he pushed a Chuck Berry CD into the player. We idled up to Walker's Cay singing Chuck Berry songs as Williams sipped his Scotch.

A couple of boat mechanics lived on a small island over from Walker's Cay. Once we got to the hotel, we used their ship-to-shore radio to contact one of them. He came over that afternoon and repaired the electronics. We were able to enjoy five days of uninterrupted fishing. It was a great trip.

This was just another day in the life of Larry Williams. I have a hundred Larry Williams stories. He was a great guy and had the best outlook on life. Nothing was going to get him down. I've seen him face adversity that no one else could even imagine. He would just let it roll off his back and keep going. People could learn a lot from Larry Williams. He was a great friend who introduced me to hunting and taught me about fishing, and more importantly, about having a good, positive attitude.

Unfortunately, about a decade ago, Larry died at the early age of sixty-nine. Way too soon.

20

WELCOME TO SONIC AUTOMOTIVE

I could tell the size and cost of the new Chevrolet Oldsmobile dealership in New Smyrna Beach was beginning to concern Dennis more and more. I think he had finally realized that the market was just not big enough to support this huge investment.

About this time, a big Ford dealer from Charlotte, North Carolina was on a crusade to buy some well-performing dealership groups so that he could package them up and start a publicly traded automobile company. This concept was just beginning, and there were already a couple publicly traded automobile companies in existence that were doing well. The dealer was Bruton Smith, a real innovative guy. A true car guy who lived and dreamed large. His company was Sonic Automotive, still today one of the largest publicly traded automobile consolidators in the United States.

Smith had just bought a group of dealerships in Chattanooga, Tennessee, from a very successful dealer, Nelson Bowers. After the deal was complete, Smith enlisted Bowers to be his point guy—the guy who would go out and beat the bushes for other groups to buy. While they would consider "one- or two-store" deals, they preferred deals with a group of four or five stores. Smith wanted to assemble a group of about thirty or so dealerships as quickly as he could. He knew you can buy four as quickly as you can buy one.

Nelson Bowers and Dennis had crossed paths somewhere over the years. Nelson knew Dennis had a group of nice, profitable dealerships and was probably approaching his late fifties by now. Nelson gave Dennis a call. Dennis met with Nelson and the new CFO for Sonic, and they worked out the framework of a deal to buy all of Dennis's stores and his finance company. The new Chevy Olds store was about six or eight months from being finished, so the timing was perfect. The Sonic people reviewed all the financial statements for the businesses and were impressed. The Chevy Olds statements were from the old facility where we were currently working. Dennis discreetly showed them the new facility and said, "Wait until this place is finished. You'll see even bigger profits." It was a nice showpiece to take back to Charlotte to show Bruton. In addition, the deal included the Mercedes store, and Bruton really wanted a Mercedes dealership to add to his collection.

Shortly after the deal was drawn up, Dennis called Trudy (his daughter running the Mercedes dealership) and me to his office. I had absolutely no knowledge this deal was in the works. We went to Dennis's office, and his longtime CPA, Brent, was there with him. He called us all back to his conference room, where a stack of notebook binders sat in front of Brent. Dennis told Trudy and me about this great offer. He said Sonic wanted both of us to stay with the company and had made us nice offers. (I'll always wonder if Trudy had some previous knowledge of the deal, and this was all a performance for me. After all, she was his daughter.) He asked us what we wanted to do. We both said we didn't want him to sell, and we would commit to being with him for the long term. After discussing it for a while, Dennis looked at Brent and told him the deal was off the table. Trudy and I went back to work.

However, the deal was never off with Dennis. It was all for show. He wasn't the one with questions or concerns about the deal. It was Sonic. He was just testing me to see if I was committed to staying with the company.

The deal was unusual. It included two domestic stores, a luxury imports store, a large stand-alone used-car store, and a finance company. All these businesses were different and required a leader who had experience in many areas. Sonic's concern was not knowing who would run the businesses after they purchased them. They knew they didn't have someone to step in and take over who already knew the pieces of the different businesses. This could have easily been a deal breaker.

I found out later that Dennis had said to Sonic, "No worries—you'll have Larry Hill."

They had asked, "Who is Larry Hill?"

Dennis sold the hell out of me. He probably oversold me. He told them how I had been with him for twenty years as his right-hand man and how I was the guy who made all these places work. He told them that half his employees didn't even know who he was when he pulled up to one of the dealerships, but they all knew me.

They asked if I would stay on with them, and he said, "Hell, yeah. He'd love to. We've already discussed it."

Now Sonic was excited about the deal again.

The only problem was, Dennis had never discussed it with me. The last time I had heard anything about the deal was the day we met in his office, and he told Trudy and me it was off. That brief meeting was his definition of us discussing it.

Sonic continued to work the deal and kept asking Dennis when they could meet with me. Dennis kept stalling. Remember, Dennis is a great salesman. He had already convinced them the Chevy Olds store would make tons of money when the new facility was finished. Nobody ever considered market size, sales potential, and expenses. They were so excited about putting this deal together that they didn't even question this. This deal would be a great payday for Dennis.

Dennis knew I was a man of integrity and honesty, and I had earned his respect over the years by never wavering on this. He didn't tell me about the deal because he was concerned, rightly so, that I would get upset and quit because of his under-the-table antics. I had earned good money working for him for twenty years. He knew I saved my money and could afford to quit and not work for years if I chose to do so. And last, he knew if I walked out the door, he didn't have a deal. He was running out of time. Sonic was coming the following Tuesday to sign the final paperwork to lock up the deal. He had to let them meet me.

On the Saturday morning before the Sonic people were to arrive, Dennis came to the dealership to see me. He was nervous as a rat. We engaged in some small talk, and then he asked if we could go to my office for a minute. By this time, the dealership had been downsized so much from the construction that I was in a tiny glass office in the middle of the dealership. It was like a fishbowl. Dennis and I are both good-sized guys, so we squeezed in, and he asked if he could close the door. He brought the deal back up, this time calling it a "merger." I guess he thought that sounded better. It was no merger. It was the same deal.

Dennis proceeded to say, "Larry, they have offered you a very nice compensation package. I think it's a good deal for you. Will you meet with them at 2:00 p.m. Tuesday at my office?"

I said, "OK." Nothing else, just "OK."

Dennis didn't like this. He wanted more communication so he could determine how I was feeling. I had deprived him of this. I said nothing more. I was confident that when he left, he was feeling more uncomfortable than when he arrived.

Tuesday at about 1:50, I headed over to his office. Sonic representatives Nelson Bowers and CFO Theo Wright were there with Dennis. Theo was your typical CFO, a non-expressive guy in a conservative business suit. Nelson is a very outgoing guy. A big guy with a big voice and a big smile. He jumped up, grabbed my hand, and shook it excitedly. He told me how happy they were to finally meet me and how many great things they had heard about me. He went on and on. A very nice guy. Theo just looked on quietly.

I sat down and said, "I very much appreciate the offer, but I am going to pass. I'm not a corporate guy. I don't think I'll mesh with the politics of a big corporation."

Then I said, "In addition, gentlemen, I just heard about this deal three days ago."

There was dead silence in the room. They both cut their eyes to Dennis. There he sat at his big desk, looking straight down at it. He never looked up at them.

I stood, shook their hands, and left the office. Damn, I would love to have heard what was said after I left.

I went back to work and focused on selling cars. That's what I do, no matter the situation. I didn't mention the meeting to anyone except my wife, Gayle, when I got home later that night.

The next day I was working in my office when the receptionist informed me that I had a call from Nelson Bowers. I asked her to transfer it to me. Nelson told me he had wanted to visit with me before he left town the evening before, but they were due in Texas that morning for a meeting. He asked if he could fly back to New Smyrna the next day to meet with me privately.

I said, "You don't have to go all that trouble. Just tell me what's on your mind."

He said, "I was very surprised to hear that you had not been told about this deal."

"I knew as much. The look on Theo and your faces clearly sent that message," I replied.

Bowers said, "Look, Larry, we need you. Give some consideration to what it would take for you to come join us. I'll call you back tomorrow morning, and you can let me know."

Gayle and I had just received the final plans for a house we were going to build on the Intracoastal Waterway in town. We were ready to begin construction. When I got home that evening, we discussed Nelson's call.

I said, "We have two choices. I can leave now and begin looking for a dealership to buy with an investor. However, keep in mind that the likelihood of us finding that opportunity within driving distance of our house is pretty slim, which would most likely require us to relocate. The other option is to see if I can put together a strong five-year employment agreement and we move forward with building the house. We could stay for at least five years, and then we decide about what to do after that."

I reminded her again that it could involve a move. We agreed to see if I could put together a good five-year deal.

Nelson called the next morning, and we agreed on the terms of a five-year employment deal. It included a clause requiring them to pay me $500,000 if they terminated me without cause during the term of the agreement. I had to make sure they weren't going to keep me just long enough to learn everything they needed about the stores, get to know my people, and then fire me to hire someone else for less money. He assured me this would not happen and assured me nothing would change. He reminded me they were paying a lot of money for these stores because of how well they performed, so they had no plans, nor did they want, to change anything.

Dennis bought back my ownership interest in the Chevy Olds store before closing.

My title was Florida Region Vice President of Sonic Automotive. I reported to a smart, nice guy named Jeff Rachor. Jeff was a well-educated business guy. We worked together well. He was a busy guy, so I didn't hear from him much, but when I did, it was usually because he wanted to send me a little praise. I enjoyed working for Jeff. I also learned a lot from him.

As the company grew and acquired more dealerships, Jeff just didn't have time to meet with all the Region Vice Presidents on any kind of regular basis. They decided to split the company into three divisions: East, Central, and West. Each division would have a Divisional VP for the Regional VPs to report to. Jeff called me when they made this decision and asked if I would have interest in being the Divisional VP for the East Division. He did say the job would require a lot of travel. In addition, I knew the position would get me closer to the politics of a big company. I thanked him for his consideration but declined.

They hired a guy from Atlanta named Lee Crumpton. Lee had the personality of a tomato but liked to give off that Clint Eastwood vibe. He was a "too cool for school" kind of guy. His recent experience had been running a big Honda dealership in Atlanta.

Running a Honda dealership in Atlanta on a major thoroughfare in the late '90s may be the easiest job in the world. Honda was probably the number-one-selling car at the time, and the store was in Atlanta. No disrespect to Lee, but a dog on the lot with a note in his mouth could sell Hondas at that location in Atlanta. Lee wanted all his Sonic stores to run like his did in Atlanta. It didn't matter the size of the market, demographics, creditworthiness of the buyers, or the make of vehicles you sold. Lee was constantly on me about my high advertising expense.

All my stores sat directly on the east coast of Florida. The Chevy Olds store and the Ford store were a mile apart, and both sat on the Intracoastal Waterway. If your dealership sits on the coast, you do not have an east market, a northeast market, or a southeast market. Therefore, you have to spend more on advertising to get deeper to the west, northwest, and southwest.

The advertising expense at all my stores had always been higher than the industry guide for this reason. Everyone who operates a store on the coast knows this is one of the disadvantages. Therefore, if you are considering buying a store on the coast, you need to know that you will spend more money on marketing. Keep in mind, as Nelson Bowers said when Sonic bought the stores, "Larry, we bought them because of how profitable they are." The high profit was in spite of the high advertising expense.

Lee struggled with this. If he wasn't sharp enough to figure this out on his own, he would clearly understand it after I explained it.

I asked him one day, after he had scolded me about our advertising expenses, to look at something. I drew a rough sketch of Florida and added a dot to represent where my stores were located. I placed a nickel over the dot and drew a circle around the nickel. This represented a twenty-five-mile radius around the area (a standard for car dealers to define their market).

Even from my rough drawing, it would be clear that 40 percent of the area was in the Atlantic Ocean. I thought this illustration would be a good way to explain it to Lee.

I said, "As you can see, 40 percent of my twenty-five-mile radius has no customers because it's in the Atlantic Ocean. I have to put more effort into reaching out to customers in the other directions."

Lee had no response to my explanation. He had pounded me for so long about it. Now it was crystal clear to him why the advertising was necessary. I think he was almost embarrassed, especially for a guy of his position, though he wasn't about to show it.

Lee had always been an odd bird. He never smiled and was very intense. One day we were on a conference call with about twenty or so of the General Managers and Regional Vice Presidents. We could hear what the dealers on the other phones lines were saying.

Lee said something, and then we heard one of the dealers on the call say, "Oh, it's Mr. Personality." Apparently, this guy had forgotten to mute his phone. No one knew who said it.

After the conference call ended, Lee called me and said, "I need you to do me a favor. I want you to find out who called me 'Mr. Personality.'"

He was so pissed off about this that he had called me and several other guys who had been on the call to get to the bottom of it. He was obsessed and continued this search for such a long time that word finally got back to Bruton Smith. Mr. Smith called Lee and told him to let it go. He was making too big of a deal out of it.

As time went on, Lee continued to pressure me to keep lowering the advertising expense, so we did. Lower advertising expense meant lower car sales, and profit suffered measurably because of it.

A short while after Dennis sold the stores to Sonic, he purchased a Mercedes dealership in Jackson, Mississippi. It's typical that sometimes after dealers sell their stores, they end up sitting around for a while thinking about it and then wind up buying another dealership somewhere. I can't say I blame them. There are benefits and perks to owning a dealership.

Trudy was still working under my direction and running the Mercedes store in Daytona after Sonic bought it, but when her dad bought the dealership in Jackson, she resigned. She and her husband relocated there so she could run the new store. I was sorry to lose her because she was a sharp operator.

I promoted Tom Pelchen, who was currently the New Car Sales Manager, to the General Manager position. He had been Trudy's right-hand guy and learned a lot from her. Typically, I visited the dealership once every couple of weeks, but I went more often when Tom first took over to help him with anything he needed to get up and running.

About a month after Trudy left, I was there when Steve Rollins, the Used Car Manager, asked if he could talk to me for a minute. He said he was going to be leaving. Steve had lived in New Smyrna Beach his entire life. He was a great, quality guy. He was a savvy investor and liked to buy real estate. He owned multiple properties around Daytona, and his wife had a good job there. I was surprised he was leaving.

He said, "I'm going to go to work for Dennis in Mississippi. He offered me a good job, a good opportunity."

I asked him if he would work until the end of the month, but Dennis had told him he needed him by the next day. I shook his hand as we parted.

I needed a new Used Car Manager, so I called Lee Crumpton the next day to ask if he had any résumés for this position. Lee had implemented a new policy that whenever a store needed to hire a Sales Manager, we had to call him first. As résumés were regularly getting sent into Sonic, they may've already had a good candidate in mind. He asked me which manager I was replacing, and I told him it was Steve Rollins at the Mercedes dealership. Lee asked where he was going, and I told him he was leaving for Mississippi to work for Dennis.

The next day, Theo Wright, the CFO of Sonic, called and was pretty hot. He said, "Larry, your Used Car Manager went to work for Dennis?"

I said, "That's what he told me, Theo."

He said, "That's a violation of Dennis's noncompete that he signed when we bought the dealerships."

"Well, Theo, I wouldn't know this," I said. "I don't know the details of Dennis's noncompete. All I can tell you is that I asked Rollins where he was going, and he told me. I would think that if Dennis knew it was a violation, he probably would have told Steve not to mention it to me."

Theo said, "You know what, Larry? He actually violated his noncompete when he took Trudy. We let it go with her because she's his daughter, but now he's really violated it."

I said, "OK, I'm sorry. I don't know what to say. I'm just looking for a Used Car Manager."

I was a little surprised that Dennis hadn't said, "Hey, Steve. Can you do me a favor? When you tell Larry you're going to leave, just don't mention where you're going." That's all he had to say.

Again, I was focused on running car dealerships and selling cars. That's all I did every day. I wasn't going to be running around trying to figure out where Steve Rollins went. The guy leaves. I don't care. I move on to the next piece.

Lee Crumpton never did send me any leads for the open position.

I promoted a guy named Hank Tulp to take Rollins's place. He had worked for us for years at the Chevy Olds dealership and was a quality guy. Hank was a perfect fit in his new position, along with Pelcher, Bruce, and the other guys. He was wired a lot like Rollins but was a little bit older, probably in his early fifties at the time. He was in good shape and worked hard. He was a good fit in that environment, and we didn't miss a beat.

Part of Dennis's package when selling the dealerships included him continuing to get the use of three vehicles—a Mercedes for his wife, one for him, and a Chevrolet truck for his son, Wallis. Word got around quickly at Sonic that Dennis had violated his noncompete. Here's what I did know: Theo Wright did not like Dennis. I didn't know if the feeling was mutual, and I didn't know what it was all about, but I knew Theo did not like him.

Theo called a few days later and said, "Larry, I need you to have Dennis's vehicles repossessed."

My heart sank. My stomach sank. I said, "What do you mean?"

"He's violated the terms of his noncompete, and we have decided we're going to take his cars. You're down there, so hire a tow service and get it handled," Theo said.

Well, I'm going to tell you, it was one of the worst days of my life, if not the worst day. It was the hardest thing anyone had ever asked of me. I had done a lot of hard things, but I didn't know how I was going to do this. Remember now, I had worked for Dennis for over twenty years and was extremely loyal. I was his right-hand guy. We were almost like family. What Theo was asking me to do was going to be beyond tough. I just so badly wanted to ask him to please handle it on his end, but I couldn't.

What I did next actually put my job on the line. I called Dennis's attorney, Larry Marsh. I told him the situation and said, "I don't know what to do. I don't want to have his cars repossessed. Please call him and tell him the situation. Ask him to call Sonic and get this worked out. I'm sick about this."

Larry said, "Gosh, I don't know what to tell you. Sounds like the big guy messed up."

Surprisingly, he was pretty open with this comment. He said he would give Dennis a call.

About a week had gone by when I received another call from Theo. He wanted to know why I hadn't had Dennis's cars picked up yet. Obviously, either Dennis hadn't talked to Sonic, or he had but they hadn't settled the matter. I felt at this point I had done all I could for Dennis. I had put my job on the line because of the loyalty I had for him.

I had no choice at this point but to call Frank Pinder, the person who ran our finance company. He was a great, smart guy. I told Frank this was the toughest thing I've ever had to tell him to do, and to keep it to himself, and then I explained to him what I needed.

He also liked Dennis, so I knew it would be hard for him as well, but he said he would get it handled.

Frank had the cars towed away three or four days later by a repossession company. They had found a window of time when all the vehicles were parked outside, as they can't be in a garage when being repossessed. Unfortunately for Dennis's son, Wallis, his trailer and boat were attached to the truck at the time.

At least the saga was over on my end.

At some point the next morning, I noticed a voicemail on my phone. I was headed into a meeting and would have to check it afterward. When I got out, there was a second message. I went back to my desk and listened to them. They were both from Dennis's son. I didn't know he had my cell number.

The first message said, "Larry, Wallis Higginbotham. Call me."

The second said, "Hey, Larry. First you have our cars repossessed, and then you don't call me back. You'd better call me. I know where you live."

I thought, *Oooh. This is interesting.* I picked up the phone and called Dennis.

I said, "First of all, I wasn't responsible for having your cars repossessed. I'd like to explain. Secondly, you probably need to reel in your son. He called me while I was in a meeting. Obviously, I couldn't get back to him as quickly as he wished, so he called again and pretty much told me that if I didn't get back to him soon, he'll come to my house."

I said, "I've got a wife and two small kids at my house. You don't want him coming to my house. If he does, let me tell you what will happen. Someone will go to the hospital, and someone will go to jail. I can't tell you which it is going to be, but that's what is going to happen."

Dennis immediately apologized for Wallis's comments. I was happy about this.

Then I said, "Dennis, I didn't have your cars repossessed."

I could tell he didn't really want to talk, so we got off the phone.

Trudy had been commuting between New Smyrna Beach and Jackson. They still had a home in New Smyrna. I had heard she was in town, so I called and asked her if she would come by the dealership to see me the next morning.

She did, and when she sat down, I said, "Look. I'm sorry about the cars, and I'm sorry about the embarrassment. I'm going to tell you what happened." I went on to explain to her the story of Rollins telling me he was going to work for her dad and that I had no idea what Dennis's noncompete stated. I told her that I simply contacted Lee Crumpton to ask if he had any leads for the open position of Sales Manager—per company policy—and that he wanted to know who was leaving and why.

I said, "Trudy, I'm sorry your dad is upset. I'm sorry what your mom and dad went through, but it wasn't my fault. I even went to the extent of calling your dad's attorney. I gave him a heads-up on what was going to happen and asked him to have your dad call Sonic to get it handled. I've been made out to be the bad guy, but this isn't the case. I have done nothing that I shouldn't have done. I hadn't told Sonic that Dennis was stealing our people. I simply answered a couple of questions."

She listened to what I said, and I appreciated this, but I could tell she was not happy. I understood this but was still disappointed because of the great working relationship she and I'd had for such a long time. She also knew of the history of loyalty I'd had to her dad. There was simply nothing more I could do. Sometimes we just have to go on down the road.

Trudy continued to run the Mercedes store in Jackson, and Steve Rollins relocated there to be the Used Car Manager.

I never knew what happened between Dennis and Sonic. I heard there had been litigation, but I didn't know what came of it, and I didn't care. It was none of my business. The relationship was pretty much over now for the Higginbothams and me. Dennis and I would cross paths at times because we lived in the same town. He would even call me occasionally, and I would call him. But the conversations were short and weren't like they'd been in the past. I wished things could have been the same because he was a big part of my life for a long time, and he'd given me many opportunities. For twenty years we had been a team, but things with Dennis and me would never be the same again.

Life went on, and I had work to do.

When I had about fifteen months left on my five-year agreement, Lee asked me to fly to Atlanta the following week for a meeting with him and Jeff Rachor. He had a driver waiting to take me to his office when I arrived at the airport. I met with them for about an hour. Jeff was the professional, polite guy, as always, and Lee was Lee. Jeff held the entire meeting. Lee didn't say anything. Sonic was about to close on three Cadillac dealerships in and around Orlando. They felt the best move was to add them to my region. We had added a dealership from Deland, Florida to my region a couple years earlier. Deland is about thirty miles from the other dealerships.

It did make sense to add the three Cadillac stores to my region, and I was fine with that; however, I reminded Jeff that I was about fifteen months out from the end of my agreement. I let him know that when it was up, I would be leaving to pursue my goal of buying my own dealership.

I said, "We will do whatever you like, but I did just want to throw that out there in the event it would impact anything."

Jeff was thankful that I was open with them. We talked for about another fifteen minutes and agreed to visit on this later. When I stood to leave, Jeff jumped right up and looked me in the eyes, as he always did, and shook my hand. Lee did not make eye contact with me. The driver took me back to the airport for my flight back to Daytona.

Lee knew I had an employment agreement but didn't know the details. He probably had come across this with some other guys during his tenure but most likely didn't realize the fee they'd have to pay me if I was terminated without cause. I'm sure this part wasn't in any of the other agreements he had seen.

A couple of weeks later, my assistant told me that Lee wanted to schedule a meeting with me for the following Monday at 5:30 in my office. I knew from experience that you fire people at the end of the day. Unfortunately, I've had to do it more times than I liked.

I said, "Tell him that's fine."

During the week leading up to that Monday, I gathered a few boxes, and after my assistant left for the day, I would box up my personal items. I parked around back so when I would leave in the evenings, I could put the boxes in my car without anyone seeing me. When I got home, I would place them in the corner of the garage. Gayle didn't notice the boxes, and I didn't mention them.

By Monday, the only personal items remaining were the items on top of my desk. When Lee arrived, he was going to share his big "surprise" and send me on my way.

Lee arrived at 5:30. My assistant had left for the day. He walked in and sat in one of the chairs in front of my desk.

No small talk—he just said, "Larry, considering you are planning to leave at the end of your agreement, we're going to make a change now."

I said, "OK, Lee. What exactly are you saying?"

He said, "You are terminated."

I stood up, now looking down on him, and said, "OK." I just continued to stare down on him, as if to say, "OK, Lee, get the hell out of my office."

He stood and left. I put the things on my desk in the last box I had tucked away and left. Lee spent the night in New Smyrna and called a meeting at the Chevy Olds store the next morning for all my General Managers. He made it clear to them that he had terminated me.

I called Jeff the next morning. He told me the original plan was for Lee and him to come see me together in hopes of working out a plan for an amicable separation. They wanted me to spend sixty or ninety days with a replacement to get him/her settled in and move forward with incorporating the Cadillac stores into the region. I would then leave, and we would negotiate the $500,000.

Jeff knew that I was a fair and reasonable person and would probably consider some form of that agreement. If not, he could then decide whether to terminate me and eat the $500,000 or allow me to stay on until my agreement was completed.

Jeff said he ended up not being able to come because he had an emergency at a new store they had just bought in Dallas. He had to be there to handle it. He had asked Lee to reschedule our meeting for later in the week, but Lee said he could handle it appropriately.

We continued to talk, and Jeff asked if it would be OK for him to meet with my General Managers and me. He would like to reinstate me for a period of three to six months to get a new Region Vice President settled in and then hand my region off to someone else.

I said, "This won't work. How is your relationship with Lee going to be when you come in and reinstate me after he fired me? Also, how am I supposed to work with him for the next three to six months after the way he terminated me?"

He agreed that his plan wouldn't work.

I reminded Jeff of the terms of my employment contract regarding termination without cause. He assured me I would be paid in full, and I was. Lee had jumped the gun and had failed in handling the meeting appropriately, as he had assured Jeff he would do. He cost Sonic $500,000. I was unemployed for the first time in my life. Wow...

21

FAMILY DYNAMICS

My mother had passed away just a couple years earlier from her alcohol abuse, and Dad lived alone in the condo they had shared in Raleigh. Now that I wasn't working, I had some time on my hands, so I went and stayed with him for a few days. We rode up to the Blue Ridge Mountains in western North Carolina to spend some time together. These times were very rare, and we both enjoyed them. Looking back, I was glad I had this opportunity to be with him.

My sister, Susan, and her husband, Wilson, had an extremely dysfunctional life. They probably would have divorced on multiple occasions if they could have afforded it. They weren't really crazy about each other, and they weren't crazy about living together, but they couldn't afford to live apart. It was a pretty tough life.

Susan struggled with her addiction to prescription medication and alcohol. This had been going on for at least twenty years. We all knew it. She had gotten caught signing a doctor's name to some prescriptions. I think she was arrested for this, but she somehow continued to get and take pills. Anyone who is addicted to drugs knows how to get them. Drugs and alcohol were just part of Susan's everyday life. She began looking worse and worse every time I would see her. I offered to send her to rehabilitation a couple of times, but she rejected my offers.

Wilson was a pretty big drinker, but he was not one to drink on the job. He was always in some type of commercial belt and hose sales business, selling those big bands on escalators or hoses for big equipment. He was working a lot of hours, sometimes twelve or more hours a day. Wilson made many poor decisions in life but seemed to be a hard worker.

They always chose to live in odd, remote places, usually in rural areas around the suburbs of Raleigh. They would occasionally drive into Raleigh to visit us. They would never be in the same car as the last visit, and the car was always beaten up and old. I don't recall except for once ever driving to any of their homes, and I don't recall Mom and Dad ever going to any of their homes, either. They were always really quiet about where they lived. It was almost like they preferred being hidden.

They never stayed in one place very long, moving around every few years. On about move number three or four, they relocated to another remote area outside of Raleigh near a lake. I use the word "lake" loosely. It was a small lake, or in reality, a big pond.

The setting had a "campground" feel, but about half of the people lived there on a permanent basis. Susan and Wilson made their home in a trailer they rented that was on a lot by the lake.

By the way they talked about this place, you would have thought they'd moved to Margaritaville or something similar. They seemed to think they were living in a luxury retirement village. They described how great it was living on the lake—this big, wonderful setting. At some point, they even got a golf cart. I don't know how they got it. They had no money. Maybe they traded something for it, or maybe they found it on the side of the road. Neither would surprise me. They would ride around the campground in the golf cart and have their cocktails.

Later, when Dad died, he left what he owned to Linda, Susan, and me. He had instructed that his assets be split equally among us. He wasn't a wealthy man, but he had worked hard and saved his money. After liquidating everything, we were all blessed with a nice check. Linda used her portion to add a new bedroom suite to her home, and as I was in the middle of a major remodel, I used mine on my home also.

Susan and Wilson blew their portion within the first year. They bought two new cars, a boat, and a travel trailer. Dad had left them enough money to purchase a nice, modest home. They had never owned a home, a place to call their own. Yet they didn't buy a home or anything that would retain value. I couldn't believe it. Every penny they had been given was spent on depreciating assets, and they remained at the little rented trailer on the small lake.

We all wanted more for Susan, for her to have a stable and loving home and environment. We continued to love her and pray for her, but there wasn't anything more we could do.

One day, after Wilson and Susan had gotten into an argument, he left to spend the weekend with their son, Jason, and his family on the coast of North Carolina. While there, he called to check in on Susan a few times, but she didn't answer the phone. He became concerned and called the local sheriff's office. He asked them to do a welfare check on her. They went to the trailer and knocked, but there was no response. After a few more tries, they broke the door in and found Susan. She had passed away in their bed from an overdose. She was fifty-three years old.

Linda and Sam continued their busy life in Raleigh with their ever-expanding family. One day, Linda and a friend decided they were going to have a garage sale. They organized the items and got everything ready to sell. Early the next morning, they opened the garage door, and the sale was off to a great start. People would walk up and ask, "How much is this?" and Linda would tell the person, "Take this with love from Jesus."

They ended up giving everything away but had a great time! They were loving it, and the people who had gone to the garage sale loved it. This garage sale and their mantra,

"Take this with love from Jesus," turned into a full-fledged ministry named "With Love From Jesus."[4]

Their ministry continued in the garage and then grew to the point where they moved it into a warehouse. In 2000, they were granted a 501(c)(3) status for their nonprofit organization and assembled a board of directors. There are some local, established businesspeople on the board. Linda is the director of the ministry, and her daughter, Leah, is Director of Operations. Through much of their lives, her children and grandchildren have volunteered.

When the ministry outgrew the first warehouse, Linda moved it into a forty-thousand-square-foot space at an old shopping center that had once been in the "hot spot" of town. The gentleman who owned the shopping center leased the various sized spaces to tenants and kept a small office there. A lot of the businesses catered to the Hispanic community. The anchor store had previously been a Walmart. There was no signage, and the old Walmart had been gutted. It was a big metal building. Hot in the summer and cold in the winter, with no heating or air conditioning, and a loading dock around back. The ministry rented this space. With

---

4. You can learn more about Linda's "With Love from Jesus" ministry at https://www.withlovefromjesus.org/. As of June 2023, With Love from Jesus was ministering to more than four thousand families each month, in addition to assisting many other ministries with helpful resources for their outreach. Each month, the ministry collects $250,000 worth of resources and gives them away freely. Donating food, household items, clothing, furniture, computers, and vehicles provides the opportunity to share the love of Christ to the community. If you're so inclined, you can make a donation.

Love From Jesus, a resource center for so many people in need, was now larger than ever!

There were many pieces to getting and keeping the resource center up and running. Trucks were donated. Old refrigerators and freezers, shelving and racks, and any products that could help with distributing food, clothing, and household items to the people were donated or negotiated to be bought as cheaply as possible.

Linda had met with the grocery stores around Raleigh and made a deal to pick up the bread, produce, meats and other groceries that were about to expire. Farmers in the area learned about the resource center and would donate any additional crops they hadn't sold. I've seen huge bushel crates of fresh corn stacked up at the warehouse, like you'd see displayed at the farmer's market.

The loading dock is used to receive these items but is also a place where people drop off things they're donating to the ministry. The donations include all types of clothing and shoes, furniture, bedding, curtains, pictures, diapers, etc. You name it, and they've probably received it. The resource center gives out an average of thirty-two hundred bags of food items and ten thousand articles of clothing each week—about 1.5 million donated items per year!

None of this would happen without Linda, the small staff, and the two-hundred and fifty volunteers. The volunteers organize the clothes, coats, shoes, and boots on racks by sizes, just like a department store, with sections for men, women, and children. They set out the furniture and arrange the household items, etc.

People line up out front, and the line is always long. Most people are repeat patrons because they have no other means to get these items.

Upon opening the doors, a few volunteers escort the first group of people into the receiving room. They hold a brief Bible study in Spanish and in English and offer to pray with anyone who is struggling with something. After this, the patrons get a cart/buggy like at a grocery store and begin shopping. There are signs in the aisles explaining how many items a person can take from each category per visit, and there are many volunteers walking around to help people.

While this is happening, the volunteers then bring in the next group of people for the brief Bible study. This keeps the traffic flow at an even pace.

Everyone involved with the resource center treats the patrons as if they were guests in their home. They are loving and kind and donate their time to keep this place running.

The ministry has grown significantly over the past twenty years. They have regular donors, including some legacy donors who have supported them from the beginning. The rent is not cheap, nor is the maintenance costs on the trucks, refrigerators, and freezers. Linda has shared with me stories about how several times they would be short of money for their rent payment, and at the last minute, a donation check would be in their post office box to cover the expense. This type of blessing is not unusual.

22

BUYING MY FIRST DEALERSHIP

After leaving Sonic, I spent the next twelve months looking for a dealership to purchase. I had a lot of free time on my hands, so I was enjoying the extra time with my daughters. Allison was in middle school, and Emily was in elementary school. I would take Allison to school in the mornings, along with two other neighbor kids, Margaret, and D. J. White. Gayle would take Emily to school. Emily and Allison, along with three of their girlfriends, took dance lessons after school some evenings about thirty minutes from the house. We had a carpool where one of the moms would drop them off at about 6:00 p.m., and another would pick them up at 8:00 p.m. I jumped into Gayle's role there while I wasn't working. All three of the moms drove white Ford Expeditions, so the girls didn't need to know who was picking them up any particular evening. They would just walk outside and get in the white Expedition.

While the girls were in school, I would spend most of my days looking for dealership opportunities. I worked with a couple different brokers. When a dealership is for sale, the seller wants it to be kept very quiet and confidential. If word gets out, employees get nervous and will start looking for other jobs. If other dealers in the seller's market hear a dealership is for sale, they will call the seller's employees and try to hire them away, telling them that the dealership they work at is for sale. A potential seller will contact a broker. These brokers usually have names of prospective buyers in the market for a car store. The broker will get the potential seller and buyer together and help facilitate the deal.

During the next twelve months, I probably looked at ten dealerships in the southeast. Some were partnership opportunities, and some dealers just wanted to sell out completely. I was open to look at any deal. I looked at a couple of Jeep Dodge Ram stores, a couple of Chevrolet stores, some other General Motors stores, a Mercedes and BMW store, and a couple of Toyota stores. I had experience with all of them and was not opposed to any if the market was right for the brand.

It can be difficult to buy a car dealership. Most car dealers have big egos. The ego can get in the way when negotiating a deal. You have to agree on the property and facility value, fixed-asset value, and goodwill value. The due-diligence process takes about six months to complete. You invest not only your time but can invest quite a bit of money in travel and in attorney and CPA fees and still not put the deal together. It just depends on how far you get into the deal and when it comes apart. They often come apart. I've seen it take dealers years to sell their dealerships. That's why confidentiality is so important. The longer one is for sale, the harder it is to keep it quiet.

About one year after I left Sonic, a broker I had been working with called me about a Ford dealership in Tennessee. He gave me enough information to check my interest level without disclosing the dealership name and location. I told him I had interest, and he sent me a confidentiality agreement to sign. Once I had signed and returned the confidentiality agreement, he sent me a copy of the dealership operating report and financial statement. The store was in Cleveland, Tennessee, in Bradley County, about twenty-five miles from Chattanooga. Cleveland is an easy drive from Chattanooga. I-75 runs through both towns, so it's a quick run up I-75 from Chattanooga. Cleveland had about forty thousand residents, and the county had about one-hundred thousand. That's a large enough market to get something going if the price is right.

I knew it would take all the money I had to get the deal done, and I didn't want to invest all my money. I had a friend who had recently sold his dealership and was retired. I asked if he would like to be a financial partner, with me having the opportunity to buy him out completely. He had interest, so we went to look at the dealership. Coincidentally, the dealership was owned by Sonic Automotive, the company that had fired me a year earlier. The dealership was losing money. Also, coincidentally, it was located in the East Division, led by none other than Lee Crumpton, the guy who had fired me. He and the several General Managers he had put in the dealership just could not make it work. After some negotiating, we put the deal together and bought the dealership. The facility was very nice, and the market was good. It had just been so poorly operated for so long that it wasn't making any money. Most Cleveland residents went to Chattanooga to buy their new Fords.

I prepared to move to Cleveland. Gayle and the girls were going to stay in Florida until the house sold or until the girls finished school that year, whichever came first. I was going to be in the dealership all the time for at least the first year anyway, so that plan worked out well. About forty-five days before we closed, Sonic announced the pending sale to the employees and allowed me to meet with them. Boy, what a sad group.

This place was in the ditch. I mean deep in the ditch. It was going to take some serious horsepower to get it out, and the group of employees I had met sure weren't going to be the group to do it. I went to see a guy I had known for years in Florida named Raleigh. Raleigh had tons of horsepower but got bored after he got a place up and going smoothly. I knew he would be the perfect guy because he would work his tail off for twelve-to-eighteen months and then would be ready to move on to the next project. He wasn't cut out for the long term, so I knew it would be a great deal. He agreed to come with me to Tennessee. We rented a two-bedroom townhouse, and we'd each go back to Florida one weekend a month. We closed the sale on October 31, 2003, and our first day of business was Saturday, November 1st. We sold three cars that day with that little rag-tag team.

We got our bearings in November and December. I bought inventory from all over the Southeast. I had to buy many new Fords from other dealers because we didn't have much inventory of our own. You earn vehicles from Ford based on what you sell, and the previous team hadn't sold much for years. We made a profit both remaining months of 2003.

We came out of the chute like a rocket on January 1, 2004. Either Raleigh or I introduced ourselves to every single customer who visited the dealership for the entire year of 2004. Nobody left until one of us had talked to them. He and I opened the dealership at 8:00 a.m. and closed it at 8:00 p.m. six days a week. On the way home from work, we had a rotation of about four restaurants that we would frequent. We would have dinner, talk about business, and then go home exhausted from the long day. If we were both in town on Sunday, we played golf.

Several of the other car dealers in Cleveland were second- or third-generation dealers. They were a little behind the times when it came to marketing and best business practices. I quickly saw some opportunity. Cleveland was, for the most part, a dual-income, 2.5-kids-per-household town. Families were tight-knit. Parents really got involved with their children's activities and their churches. Cleveland was known as the "buckle" of the Bible Belt. I came to know some fine pastors in town. I began partnering up with some of the churches to do fundraisers. We would send the youth on mission trips and help raise money to enhance the youth departments.

Cleveland was a huge high school football town. There were three high schools. If you wanted to find anybody in town on a Friday night in the fall, you would go to one of the high school football games. I had heard this, so a couple weeks after we opened, I went to a Cleveland High vs. Bradley High game. The stadium was packed with students, families, and friends of the players, along with all the faculty. The games had very good announcers. Steve Hartline, the owner of a local radio station, was frequently the announcer. Steve was born with that great announcer voice. We became good friends. I could picture Steve doing advertising spots for me. I went to each of the high school principals or athletic directors and asked if I could sponsor the games for a nice contribution to their football programs. All three of the schools jumped on board. Before you knew it, we were getting two plugs per quarter during each game. Ole Steve would say, "Tonight's game is brought to you by your hometown Ford dealer, Larry Hill Ford." The sleepy little Ford dealership that could never get anything going in Cleveland was now on the radar.

The three high schools offered drivers' education classes but no driving training. The schools didn't have the budget for cars. Although the kids could take the class, they still couldn't get their learners' permits until they had completed the driving portion. This was usually at the parents' expense through a private teaching service. I gave each of the schools one or two new Fords for driving training. One of the coaches provided the training. I had nice vinyl letters installed on the sides of the cars that read, "This Driver Training Vehicle is Courtesy of Larry Hill Ford." I only required that they keep them clean and have them parked in front of the school drop-off circle every morning when parents were bringing the children to school. I received more appreciation via calls and emails for supplying these cars than anything else I ever did for the community.

We also began a nice Christmas tradition the second year we were in Cleveland, and it was very much appreciated. There were ten fire houses in the county—five city houses and five county houses. Each had three shifts of firefighters who worked twenty-four hours and then had forty-eight hours off. I would order a big box of food from Panera Bread for each department, with enough food to serve all three shifts. There was enough food for the Christmas Eve shift, the Christmas shift, and the day-after-Christmas shift. My daughters and wife would drop them off on Christmas Eve. Once the girls were old enough to drive, they would don their Santa hats and do it themselves.

One day, a young Cleveland police officer died in the line of duty. He left behind a wife and three young children. It was the first time since the mid-1970s that an officer in Cleveland had died in the line of duty. We had a big sale scheduled at the dealership for the following weekend. I made the decision to donate $100 for every vehicle we sold to the police officer's family. On Monday morning, we were all excited for her to get a nice check.

During my time in Cleveland, we were hit by two tornadoes. Both times, the dealership provided financial assistance for local victims through the American Red Cross. Cleveland didn't have a Red Cross chapter, so I made the donation through the Chattanooga Red Cross chapter with the stipulation the funds be used for tornado victims in the Cleveland area. When I called the office to make the first donation, the representative was very appreciative and mentioned that no other car dealer in the Chattanooga area had offered any support. Then months later, when a second tornado came through, I called the same office with a second donation. Each American Red Cross chapter offers an annual "Hometown Hero Award" that goes to a person or a business that has offered significant support to the Red Cross. That year, Larry Hill Ford was the Chattanooga American Red Cross Hometown Hero.

We continued doing more things for the community during my time there. I sponsored golf tournaments for several local churches and got involved in as many civic activities as possible.

Sometimes I think back to an interesting conversation I had a couple of weeks before we closed on the dealership. I had called a Regional Sales Executive with Ford who oversaw the Cleveland area. I introduced myself and said I was about to take over the dealership. He became very quiet. I thought for a minute that we had lost our connection. Then he spoke. He said, "Larry, you are about to buy the biggest piece of s--- of a dealership I have ever seen."

I was dumbfounded. This was an executive with Ford Motor Company whom I was now representing. Not quite the welcome I was expecting. He went on to say that of all the dealerships in his region, this was his biggest pain in his ass. He said, "It's a terrible store. It has terrible people, and I can't believe you bought it." Six months later, he was on the showroom floor of the dealership, shaking my hand as hard as Nelson Bowers had done that day five years earlier in Dennis's office in New Smyrna Beach. I thought he was going to dislocate my arm while telling me how great I was. Ha.

We still had a couple tough competitors in town, but we eliminated most of them in short order. Very few, if any, of the local dealers were involved in the community. Quite frankly, I would see these dealers and their sons and daughters who were born and raised in that neat town and wonder why they hadn't been doing this stuff for years.

Our house in Florida sold, and Gayle and the girls moved to Cleveland in April 2004. We had purchased a house in the Cleveland Country Club neighborhood a couple of months before and were in the process of renovating, but it wasn't yet completed. I moved Raleigh into a small one-bedroom apartment in town. My family moved into the townhouse, where we stayed until the house was finished in August. We enrolled the girls in school for the upcoming year. We were back to a much more normal life.

Back at the dealership, we just kept taking care of customers any way we could, and our business continued to improve. I would have a private giggle occasionally when I thought about how things had come full circle. Lee had fired me from Sonic, and now we were killing it at the Ford dealership he couldn't make work.

Early in 2005, Raleigh decided he was ready to go back to Florida. He had been a huge help, and I appreciated every single day he gave me at the dealership. We had the dealership out of the ditch now, and I was able to build a good long-term team around what Raleigh and I had done together during those first fifteen months.

We continued to grow and prosper in Cleveland. One day I got a call from my direct contact with Ford, a great lady named Nicole.

Nicole said, "Hey, you've done so well turning that Cleveland store around, I was wondering if you are ready for another project."

We talked a bit, and she told me about a dealership located fifteen minutes or so outside Knoxville in Lenoir City, Tennessee. It was a carbon copy of the Cleveland store when we had bought it – under performing and not profitable.

The man who owned the Lenoir City store owned fourteen dealerships. Most of them were Nissan or other import stores. When I called him, he made it clear that he did not like Ford or any other domestic dealerships. His office was in New Jersey, and he was a tough character. Every other word he spoke was a curse word.

He told me that his General Manager in Lenoir City was aware of the fact he wanted to sell the dealership, and he would put me in touch with him. Shortly after, the General Manager called and invited me to go look at the dealership.

I made the hour drive from Cleveland, met with the General Manager, and then proceeded to take a look around at the store. My first thought was, *Man, what a piece of junk.* It was, however, located on the main four-lane highway in Lenoir City (which has now been expanded to six lanes), just one mile from I-75. Again, there were so many similarities between it and the Cleveland store.

I called my partner, Fred, to see if he had interest in us buying the dealership together if we hired a Managing Partner to run it. He had interest, and after the due diligence was completed, we closed on it in June 2006. A friend had referred a potential Managing Partner to me whom I interviewed and eventually hired to operate the dealership. He did an "OK" job, but not a great job. The dealership did not perform nearly at the level as Larry Hill Ford in Cleveland did. However, it was still a good investment for Fred and me.

23

STRUGGLES AT HOME

I had bought the home we were currently in soon after purchasing the dealership in Cleveland. It had always been considered a transition home, not our long-term place. After a while, Gayle began looking at houses and found one she really liked. It fit our family better. We remained in our original home while we did major renovations to it.

The new house was located in an older, established neighborhood with larger homes and huge, mature trees. From the road, all you could see of our house were two big brick columns, a wrought-iron gate, and a long driveway that meandered down through the woods. About six or seven hundred feet from the entrance sat our home on ten acres. It had a three-car detached garage with a guest apartment above, a gentlemen's barn, and a fenced corral. There was a two-acre lake with a big deck connecting the lake to the house. It was a peaceful setting.

One day, a black Labrador wandered up to the back door. He was a nice-looking dog with no collar or tags. He appeared to be healthy and well groomed. He showed up each evening for a few days. The girls fed him, and he continued to hang around the house. We asked the neighbors if anyone knew anything about him. No one did. The girls took him to the vet to be checked for a microchip. There was no chip, so we decided we would adopt him.

We had an invisible fence installed around two acres of the property. This gave him plenty of room to play and enjoy the outdoors while keeping him confined to the yard. We named him Buddy.

He stayed outside during the day, but we let him come inside the back den at night. That is where the kids would do their homework and watch TV. Buddy settled in nicely.

I really bonded with Buddy. He would hang around with me when I was outside doing chores. I had one of those "gator" utility vehicles that I used around the property. As soon as I would start it up, he would jump in the front seat next to me. He could spend all day in that gator.

I really looked forward to Sunday mornings. Sunday was the only day I didn't work. We would frequently attend Westwood Baptist Church, where we were members. I would get up each Sunday morning well before time to go to church, when it was still dark. This particular time before the others got up was always very special to me. I would turn the coffee pot on and walk with Buddy down the driveway to the gate to get the Sunday paper. Upon returning to the house, I'd pour a cup of coffee and go sit in the den with my newspaper.

Gayle was doing a great job with the girls while I was working a lot. She was a great mom. She took the girls with her everywhere she went. They seemed to be doing great. Allison was still involved in dance, Emily was involved in cheerleading, and both enjoyed activities at our church.

When living in Florida, Gayle and I had experienced some marital problems and had been seeing a counselor off and on for a while. We both knew the importance of working on a marriage. In Cleveland, our marriage was struggling as well, so we started seeing a great counselor we found in nearby Chattanooga.

Gayle's behavior was changing more and more as time passed. One day, a good friend of mine was telling me about the effects of his wife's bipolar condition. As he spoke, I felt as if he was describing Gayle. Gayle had been seeing a mental health provider, Dr. Lilly, for some of her issues. One morning, when we were alone in the kitchen, I took the opportunity to discuss it with her.

I asked, "Has Dr. Lilly ever mentioned 'bipolar disorder' to you?"

Gayle calmly looked up at me and said, "Why don't you worry about you, and I'll worry about me?"

I knew clearly the conversation was over. I said, "Fine" and left for work.

About two weeks later, we were again in the kitchen when she said, "Dr. Lilly said I have bipolar two disorder."

I said, "Really? Tell me about it."

She never mentioned the comment I had made about it a couple weeks before, and I wasn't sure she even remembered it. Dr. Lilly told her the disorder was very treatable but required some work. The medications called "cocktails" had to be changed up frequently. It was imperative for her to keep her appointments. Gayle seemed encouraged.

From time to time, I noticed there were bills from Dr. Lilly for missed appointments. I also knew Gayle wasn't taking her prescriptions regularly because she would mention out loud sometimes, "Oh gosh, I forgot to refill my so-and-so" or "I've run out of my so-and-so."

I could tell she was struggling. I honestly felt bad for her. She knew I was there for her, but she had made it clear that I was not to get involved unless she asked.

Gayle and I had the habit of going out to dinner for a date night on Saturdays. This dated back to our early years in New Smyrna. Gayle did not drink. We would go to dinner every Saturday night, and I would have two glasses of wine or two beers. We would usually stop by Walmart or Lowe's on the way home. We had done this for over fifteen years.

One day she said, "I don't want to ride with you when you have had any alcohol."

I told her this was fine, and we agreed she would drive on Saturday nights.

The next Saturday night, we went to Café Roma in Cleveland, a great Italian spot. I had my two glasses of wine. When we went out to the car, we were both at the passenger side. It was cold.

She said, "Hurry up. Let me in, I'm freezing."

I said, "You're driving, remember?"

She said, "Oh, yeah" and hurried around to the driver's side. I could tell she was uncomfortable driving home. I don't know why, but she was just unsettled.

The next week, she said, "I'm not driving tonight. That is enabling you."

I again told her this was fine. We went to dinner, and I had no wine. This went on for a couple weeks.

One evening when I got home after work, Gayle was lying out on the back patio, almost in a meditation fashion, flat on the stone floor.

She said, "I don't want you keeping wine in the house anymore."

I usually kept one or two bottles at home and would occasionally have a glass in an antique glass she had bought me for wine. The next morning, I took the wine with me and gave it to a friend.

We took the girls to Daytona Beach a couple weeks later for a short spring-break trip. A friend of mine, Glenn, and his wife, Cathy, owned a very nice condo on the beach there. They used it in the summer for family vacations or to get away on the weekends from their home in Melbourne, Florida. They offered to let us use it for our stay. I told Gayle that I wanted the two of us to take the forty-five-minute drive to Melbourne one night while we were there and treat them to dinner to thank them for their kindness.

She agreed, so we got the girls pizza one evening and left for Glenn and Cathy's. On the way down, I mentioned to Gayle that I was going to have a cocktail or two with Glenn at dinner. He rarely drank, but when we went out to dinner, we both enjoyed a couple of drinks.

Gayle turned quickly to me and said, "I don't condone driving while drinking, and you will not have a cocktail."

We arrived at Glenn and Cathy's house and got in Cathy's car to go to dinner. Glenn drove us to dinner, He had two Crown Royals with Diet Coke, and I had water. We all got back in the car, and he drove us back to his house.

Gayle never said, "Hey, Glenn, I noticed you had a couple cocktails during dinner. Do you mind if Cathy or I drive back to the house?" She said nothing.

On our way back to the condo after leaving Glenn and Cathy's house, we had an argument. I told her I was unhappy with her making rules instead of having conversations with me and then changing the rules whenever she wanted. I was unhappy that she expected me to go along with this protocol and how she didn't condone drinking and driving but was fine riding with Glenn and saying nothing when she knew he'd had two drinks. I told her I was beginning to feel like a pawn in some silly game she was playing.

Needless to say, it was not a pleasant ride home. Things had finally come to a head. The next day, we packed up and returned to Cleveland as planned.

A few days later, I wrote Gayle a letter. I told her that making "rules" any time she felt the need and expecting me to go along with them, and then changing them once she thought of something else, wasn't going to work. I went on to tell her that I thought her unhappiness was not due to me. Something else was the cause, and I was tired of being blamed for her unhappiness.

Yes, we both knew I worked too many hours, but she'd always known it was part of the retail car business. Nothing had changed with this in our twenty-plus years together. I lived a healthy life, was a man of integrity, and I took good care of her and our daughters.

I told her if the marriage was to continue, she would have to agree to no longer blame her unhappiness on me. She would have to show up for her appointments with Dr. Lilly and also agree to ongoing marriage counseling with me to keep us on track. I left the note in an envelope on the kitchen table and went to work.

The following Sunday, I had to leave for a Ford meeting in Michigan. The girls had gone to church, and just Gayle and I were at the house. As I was preparing to go to the airport, she asked if I wanted to discuss the letter.

I said, "Absolutely."

She sat across the room from me with a very stern look on her face and said, "I'll go to my doctor appointments when I want, and I have no interest in doing further counseling with you."

I said, "OK, fine." I grabbed my bags and left for the airport.

On the way, I called a friend of mine who is an attorney and said, "I want a divorce. Please handle it."

Gayle and I decided to wait two months until school was out for the summer before telling the kids. Allison was a senior and would be headed to college at Belmont University in Nashville in the fall. Emily was a sophomore in high school.

We still owned the original house we had bought when moving to Cleveland. I spent the next few weeks getting some furnishings in the house so I could move in when the time came.

When school ended, we sat the girls down and told them. It was the saddest day of my life. They cried hysterically. We all cried. It was horrible. My biggest concern at that time was Allison. She was leaving for college and was so lonely. She was leaving home for the first time while also trying to process her parents' divorce. I hurt so badly for Allison.

I hurt for Emily also, but I felt some relief knowing she would still be around and we could keep an eye on her. I spent as much time as I could with her. Although she and I have never discussed this, I really felt she was a bit of a rock for her mom during those early days. She was a bit of her mom's caretaker. Although Gayle was a wonderful mom, I think the girls knew a little more about her struggles than I had realized at the time. This is simply my belief. The girls have always been very supportive of their mother.

Buddy stayed there with Gayle and Emily. My house did not have a fenced yard. Plus, I was at work most of the time, so it only made sense to leave him. Also, I thought he may be a good companion for Emily.

The divorce was finalized in January 2009. Emily and I had dinner a couple times a week, and she occasionally slept over at my house. I had completely furnished a room for Emily and a room for Allison. I wanted them to know that it wasn't just my home; it was our home.

24

LARRY HILL IMPORTS

I had an opportunity to open a third business. I purchased the closed-down Chrysler Jeep dealership next door to Larry Hill Ford. After months of renovations, we opened Larry Hill Imports. I stocked it mostly with fairly new pre-owned import vehicles that we would buy at auctions all over the Southeast. Within a year, we were selling over one hundred vehicles per month there.

After Raleigh left, I replaced him with a great car guy I had known for years named Chris Sather. Chris was the General Sales Manager at Larry Hill Ford. When I opened Larry Hill Imports, I offered Chris an ownership stake in the new business, and he accepted. Now Chris was overseeing the entire sales and finance operations for Larry Hill Ford, Larry Hill Ford Pre-Owned Vehicles, and Larry Hill Imports. He had a big job and was good at it.

Our dealerships had fought the economic meltdown of 2008, and we were still battling it when I got divorced. Fortunately, we got through better than many others. The industry started to turn around in 2010. I was still buying down Fred's interest in Larry Hill Ford at that time.

Again, both 2008 and 2009 were tough years in the car business. General Motors and Chrysler had filed for bankruptcy protection and went to Washington to petition Congress for a bailout. Ford was on the fence and ended up not filing. After months of negotiations between the automakers and Congress, the government agreed to give GM and Chrysler a loan to stay in business.

Although Ford made it through the crisis without the government loan, had General Motors and Chrysler gone bankrupt, Ford most likely would have also because the Big Three used many of the same vendors and suppliers. If the suppliers had lost GM and Chrysler, they likely would have failed also because Ford alone could not have kept them in business.

I have always been a strong used-vehicle operator. I learned the importance of used-vehicle sales when working for Dennis Higginbotham. When new-vehicle sales get tough, you can always alter your used inventories to match market needs and conditions.

We were selling between one-hundred and seventy-five and two hundred used vehicles per month between Larry Hill Ford and Larry Hill Imports. We would sell about seventy new Ford vehicles. There were several months when we sold well in excess of three hundred total vehicles. We had done a good job of penetrating the Chattanooga market, as well as even selling into Georgia and North Carolina.

On Mondays, Chris would spend most of the day online, researching various auctions, looking for specific vehicles we needed. He would determine the best two or three auctions for us to attend that week. He would give Mike, our buyer, his plane tickets and give him instructions on what he needed to buy.

Mike was a great buyer. He would grab the Monday-night flight from Chattanooga and head to his destination. He would buy what vehicles he could there and then fly out for Wednesday's auction.

Transport trucks full of vehicles would start arriving at the dealership a few days later. I used to tell Chris that he could go through a half a million dollars quicker than anyone I knew.

He'd laugh and say, "It's only money." He was a great car guy.

Lenoir City Ford made it through 2008–09 also, but even before this time, we realized the original operator we had hired just wasn't the right fit and needed to be replaced. Although our second operator, Jim, did a better job than his predecessor, he still never got the store above a five or a six on a scale of ten, but he ran it with professionalism and integrity. This was my primary objective, and again, it was still a good investment.

25

A PRETTY REALTOR

When I moved back to our original house after the divorce, I had the same Sunday-morning routine with the newspaper and coffee.

When reading the newspaper, I'd always check out the real estate section. I was still relatively new to the Tennessee Valley and liked to monitor home prices in the Cleveland/ Chattanooga area. This section became familiar to me, and I would frequently see the same faces. You could tell by their ads which agents were selling a lot of property in the market. One of the faces I began to recognize was that of a pretty Realtor by the name of Jill Kisling. I could tell by her look, attire, and smile that she was a real Southern lady. She was very pretty and always had lots of nice listings.

A friend of mine and his wife were always trying to set me up with dates after my divorce. I told them more than once that I was focused only on my business and my daughters. There would be time for dates later.

One day, my friend was talking about a piece of property he was going to look at later that week in Chattanooga. I wasn't really paying much attention to what he was saying as he rambled on about the property. The following Monday night, he and I were having dinner, as we always did after our weekly men's group meeting. He mentioned that he had looked at the property with a Realtor acquaintance from Chattanooga. He went on to say that he had "forgotten how pretty Jill was." That got my attention. All I really heard was "Realtor," "pretty," and "Jill."

I said, "What is Jill's last name?" I could not remember her last name because it was a bit unusual, but as soon as he said "Kisling," I remembered it.

I said, "What is her marital status?" He told me that she was recently divorced.

I said, "I'll go out with her." Ha.

We continued our Monday-evening tradition of attending our men's group meeting and having dinner afterward. The subject of me wanting to go out with Jill didn't come up again. I assumed he had forgotten or maybe he had said something to her and she wasn't interested or whatever.

Several weeks later, I was leaving the dealership in Lenoir City one afternoon, heading back to Cleveland, and my friend called.

When I answered, he said, "We're having dinner with Jill Saturday night."

He and his wife knew Jill from the Baylor School in Chattanooga. Both he and Jill sent their children there, and they had met through school activities. He called Jill and asked if she would join his wife and him for dinner with a friend of theirs. He said she reluctantly agreed.

Although I was excited about having dinner, I didn't go into it with any great expectations after he said she "reluctantly" agreed. She had made it clear she didn't want it to be "a date."

We went to her house the following Saturday night. She was there with her middle child, Sophia, a junior at Baylor. We sat and visited for a bit, enjoyed a glass of wine, and then went to dinner. This was both my and Jill's first date since our divorces. We both had a great time, and we dated exclusively for the next two and a half years.

Jill had been married twice as well. She had two children, Whitfield and Sophia, from the first marriage and then Annabel from her second.

I continued to live in Cleveland and Jill in Chattanooga during our courtship. She and I both had busy careers, and we would see each other on weekends.

Larry Hill Ford and Larry Hill Imports continued to improve and grow every year. I think one of the best decisions I ever made was not to pull back with my marketing during the downturn. I continued to advertise with the frequency that I had before, and I continued to stay involved in all my community-support projects and initiatives.

While most car dealers were pulling back the reins during these turbulent times, I held the pedal to the metal just as if I didn't know the economy was in the dumpster. We never discussed the "recession" or had any conversation about tough times in staff or sales meetings at the dealerships. Therefore, when the economy did come back, we had so much energy behind us that we sailed to the top. That bad period was nothing more than a blip on the radar screen for us.

Our continuing community-service efforts during the downturn paid off in several ways. First and foremost, the community benefited and appreciated it. Secondly, Ford Motor Company recognized it.

Ford's highest award offered to its dealers is a worldwide award called the "Salute to Dealers Award." It is presented to six Ford dealers worldwide each year based on their community support and humanitarian efforts in their markets. Dealers are nominated by personnel from their local regional offices. We were in the Atlanta Region, which accounted for about 150 Ford dealers.

There are more than ten thousand Ford dealers in the world. While I did not receive one of the six awards, I did receive a nice letter from Edsel Bryant Ford II, a great-grandson of Ford Motor Company founder Henry Ford, saying that I was one of the eighty-one dealers worldwide who had been nominated.

Fewer than 1 percent of the world's Ford dealers were nominated, and Larry Hill Ford in Cleveland was one. That nomination ranks as the accomplishment of which I am most proud.

We had a long wall at the Ford dealership that ran from the Sales Department to the Service Department. We called it our "Wall of Fame." The wall was covered with awards, citations, newspaper articles, and accolades we had received over the years for our community service. Ford executives were amazed when they would come to the dealership and see the wall. On a visit one day, the Atlanta Region Manager saw the wall and asked me if I credited our success to our huge community involvement. I said I felt it was one of the many important pieces of the puzzle.

The years 2008–09 were also a tough time for Realtors; however, Jill had done so well in the years leading up to this period that she sailed through as well. Jill and I were both veterans of our industries. It wasn't our first rodeo, so we went into the downturn with experience under our belts.

It was very important to Jill and me that our children fit well together. Once our relationship began to get serious, this became a frequent topic of discussion. With Allison and Whitfield in college, Emily living in Cleveland, and Sophia and Annabel in Chattanooga, there just weren't many times we could get everyone all together. After about eighteen months of dating, Jill and I decided we would take them all to the Bahamas. This would be like a little dry run, if you will, to see how everyone got along.

At the hotel, Jill and her children shared a room, and Allison, Emily, and I shared a room. We enjoyed the beach, pool, spa, snorkeling, and golf during our stay.

A few days earlier, upon arriving, we had taken a shuttle ride from the airport to the hotel and had passed a cool-looking local church. We decided we would like to go to a service there. We didn't know exactly what time church would begin, so we planned to all meet at one of the hotel restaurants for breakfast the following Sunday morning and leave from there. Unfortunately, this was the extent of the "planning" we did for this particular event.

After breakfast, I walked out front to the valet and asked if they could have the shuttle take us to church. One of them informed me that the shuttle was on an airport run and wouldn't be back for about an hour. Then he checked the time for the church service and said it would be starting in fifteen minutes.

I quickly looked around the parking lot, searching for a vehicle large enough to carry the seven of us. There sat a big black stretch limousine parked over to the side with the driver standing next to it.

I realized that I had not brought my wallet with me to breakfast, and with the size of the hotel, and the time crunch we were on, I wouldn't be able to go back to the room to get it. However, I did have $83 in my pocket.

I asked the driver how much he would charge to take us on the 10-minute ride to the church and pick us back up an hour later for a previously scheduled event.

He said he would do it for $100. Welcome to the Bahamas…

I pulled my cash out and said, "All I have is eighty dollars." (I didn't even bother mentioning the other three one-dollar bills).

He reluctantly said, "OK, mon.. I'll do it." Ha.

We all jumped in, and away we went to the church.

Upon arriving, we saw there were several nice Bahamian ushers out front welcoming the members and guests. When we pulled up, a couple of them immediately came over to the limo and welcomed us. They escorted the seven of us out of the limo and into the church and then whisked us all the way down the aisle to an empty *front-row pew*.

We were all a little surprised that the front row was available, totally empty, in this almost-full church. I could see the children giving each other "looks," a little embarrassed that we were now the center of attention. I had pictured us just quietly stepping in and grabbing a seat in the back to enjoy the local church service experience.

The church was packed with locals. The music was loud, and everyone was standing with their arms raised to the sky, engaging in praise and worship. I knew we'd look back on this one day and remember what a beautiful and special time it had been for us.

As the praise and singing continued, one of the pastors came to me with a piece of paper and pen and asked me to write down all our names. I did so and returned the paper to him.

We became aware of the time, as we knew we had only one hour to be there. The singing had gone on for so long that in just a few minutes, the driver would be there to get us. We hadn't even gotten to the sermon yet.

When the singing did finally stop and everyone sat down, the pastor pulled out the paper and introduced each of us by name—the special guests who had arrived at the Bahamian church in a stretch limo.

We were past nervous at this point and looking back and forth at each other with wide eyes, glancing toward the back of the church to the far-away doors. How were we going to make it down the aisle from the front pew, passing every single person in that church, and just walk out before the service had ended?

Now, to make matters worse, they began passing around the offering bags. Keep in mind, I, Mr. Big Shot, had three one-dollar bills in my pocket. Thank goodness it was a closed bag rather than an open plate. I was able to slip the three bills down into the bag without anyone seeing the amount.

Somehow, we did end up making a silent game plan to leave. We all stood up at the same time and walked out of there to catch our ride. The walk of shame. We were humiliated.

What a memorable Sunday morning. Just not the memories I thought we'd have!

Jill and I were married in the summer of 2011. We had dated for over two years. We had a small wedding performed by our good friend, Pastor Tim Tinsley, at First Presbyterian Church of Chattanooga with only our children in attendance. It was very special.

We loved getting to know Tim during premarital counseling, and Jill became good friends with his wife, Laura. Sadly, Tim passed away about ten years later with pancreatic cancer. It was such a sad time, and everyone still misses Tim's wisdom and humor.

All five of our children meshed well or we would not have continued dating at the beginning. They had to fit well for Jill and I to fit well. Their relationship was as important to us as our own. They are all good kids. They made good grades, didn't get into trouble, had good friends, and were well educated. Most importantly, they loved each other. They still do. I have never heard any of them refer to the others as "step" brother or sisters. They simply introduce the others as their sisters or brother. We are blessed.

Sophia had graduated high school and was at college the year before we married, but Annabel was still at Baylor, so Jill and Annabel continued to live in their home in Chattanooga. I continued to live at my same house in Cleveland. We lived together on weekends. Annabel was her father's only child. She stayed with him every other weekend. He was and always had been very involved in her life. He was a good dad to Annabel, just as Gayle had always been a good mom to Allison and Emily.

The following year, Jill and I built a new home together in Chattanooga and moved in, along with Annabel. Life was great, and business was good. Jill and I were busy with our businesses and the five children coming and going. Not "too" busy, I must have thought, because this was the year that I decided I wanted another dog.

At that time, Whitfield was at the University of Tennessee in Knoxville. Sophia was at Lee University in Cleveland. Allison was about to graduate from Belmont University and begin her master's program at the University of Tennessee. Emily was at the University of Tennessee in Chattanooga, and Annabel was a senior in high school. With the last child about to leave for college in a few months, Jill and I would have weekends alone together and time to travel for the first time since we had met.

The timing of my wanting a dog was going to throw a wrench in these plans. Convincing her that this was a good idea was going to be one of the hardest sales pitches of my life.

26

MY BEST FRIEND

The whole "wanting a dog thing" started when Jill and I took Emily and Annabel on a weekend trip to Lake Oconee a couple of years after we were married. The Ritz Carlton there at Reynolds had a beautiful, old chocolate Lab named Dooley who sat by the concierge stand. I assumed he was named after the legendary University of Georgia football coach, Vince Dooley.

He was a sweet dog. I asked the concierge about him and found out he was a rescue dog from the Atlanta Lab Rescue (ALR) that they had adopted. Each night, one of the employees took him home and cared for him, but he was on the job every day, welcoming guests to the hotel.

After the trip, I started researching Labs at ALR. I didn't mention the idea to Jill.

I would see various Labs come and go on the site. There would be a few pictures of each dog with a little biography, age/or approximate age, known health conditions if any, and a remark about the dog's disposition. After a couple of months, I found a dog I really had interest in meeting. He was a four-to-five-year-old black American Lab, weighing approximately fifty pounds. Not a young puppy, and not too large. He was very similar to my old dog, Buddy, and his name was Buddy!

Once a month, the agency would hold a "meet and greet" at an Atlanta-area shopping center parking lot, where they would take all the dogs. I finally had to discuss my idea with Jill.

There are two versions of the story. Jill had agreed to at least give my idea of getting a dog consideration. We went to Atlanta on the weekend that the dogs were going to be brought to the event. There were probably thirty or so dogs on this particular Saturday. I walked around the area, checking out each dog, petting some, and looking for the one I had found online that I wanted to meet. Jill sat on a bench at the edge of the viewing area, shaking her head, still not believing we were actually considering doing this. *This part* of the story, we both agree happened. Where the story varies is the following.

My version: I walked around observing the dogs, not having interest in any of them as I was looking for the dog from the website I had come to meet. Finally, after not being able to find him, I asked the director if she could point me in the right direction. She told me the foster parents weren't able to bring him that day for whatever reason. I was disappointed and ready to go home and decided I would try again at a later date. Jill walked up to me and said she found a dog she wanted. I went over to check him out. He was a beautiful Lab mixed breed. He was white—as in solid, bright white—and stunning. He stood proud and still and wasn't barking or roughhousing like the other dogs. He almost seemed regal and a tad embarrassed that he was there with those other misbehaving dogs. I agreed we would get him.

Jill's version: She had no interest in getting a dog at this point in our lives, so she sat on the bench, randomly observing the event while I walked around looking at the dogs, trying to find the one I had come to see. It was somewhat of a chaotic scene. It was very loud, with all the dogs barking, jumping, pulling on their leashes, and vying for attention. One dog continued to catch her eye because he was not only strikingly beautiful, but he was also calm. His demeanor was peaceful. Jill could tell he wasn't participating in any foolishness, and this didn't change the entire time she watched him. He never barked. He stood tall and looked forward the entire time she watched him. She knew by then that I was disappointed the dog I originally wanted wasn't there, yet I still continued to look for one to choose. She finally said to me, "If you have to get a dog, just get that one over there. I've been watching him, and he seems special. Super chill and different from the others."

To this day, I think she wanted to get that dog, and to this day, she said she thought I was getting one anyway, so she simply pointed out this one to me. No matter, we left with a dog.

Because he was a rescue with no history, we didn't know his name. We were going to have to choose one. We tried out many on him, and his name changed every day for the next three or four days. We tried Buffett, Jake, and Max. There may have been more, but I do remember these. None of them seemed to fit him.

Each morning, I would say, "Come on, (whatever his name was that day), let's go outside." Then I would grab his leash and say, "Let's go, Buddy." I would say "Buddy" as a nickname or a term of endearment. We would catch ourselves always calling him Buddy instead of the name we were testing as an option.

After the third or fourth day, I told Jill and Annabel that we should just name him Buddy. Although I'd had a Buddy previously, we decided it would be fine, so we chose the formal name of Buddy II. He went by the name Buddy, or any variation of this, such as Bud, the Budster, or Stersy. We would spend almost a decade with this amazing, intelligent, loving, and wise human-like dog. He never left our sides—and I mean he never left our sides.

We could go anywhere, and he would stand beside us and never run away. After a while, we stopped using the leash because it just wasn't necessary.

After buying our home in Ponte Vedra, he fell right into the routine of traveling back and forth with us several times a year. He had everything he needed at both houses, so he was very comfortable, and he had neighborhood friends at both homes who were always excited to see him.

Buddy was a homebody. Although very friendly to other dogs and people, he didn't feel the need for a lot of playing. Jill and I always felt he thought all that "playing around" was just unnecessary foolishness. When other dogs or people approached him, he would smell for a second, maybe one quick lick on their face, then head off to be by himself. If another dog wanted to play, he would just respectfully walk away. He had no interest.

We have said for years that Buddy would be the happiest animal ever if the world existed of only him and our family. That was all he needed.

Buddy and I were much alike in the sense that we weren't big socializers. I think my tendency to not feel the need for crowds goes back to the alone time I spent as a kid on Lead Mine Road. I don't know what Buddy's excuse was. However, we were alike in that sense. We were both very happy and content just hanging out with each other.

One of his favorite activities was to ride around the neighborhood in Ponte Vedra in the back seat of the golf cart. He loved standing on the back-seat floor and hanging his head out to blow in the wind, but he mainly loved standing up in the back seat and "surfing" on all fours. No matter how fast we went or how we took the turns, he rode proud and strong and never fell. People stared and pointed at him, and he loved it, I could tell.

He was just so well behaved. He loved to go to Home Depot with me. Dogs are welcome in Home Depot, and I would go frequently. I would park my truck or golf cart, and we would both just get out and walk in. No leash was necessary. He never left my side. He would walk through the parking lot with me, and when I stopped at the crossing to check for traffic, he would stop and look both ways, just like me.

It amazed people when they saw him do this. We would walk through Home Depot next to each other. When people would walk up to pet him, he would not acknowledge them. He would just keep to himself, walking next to me. However, he would stop whenever one of the employees asked if he could have a treat.

I would say, "It's OK, Buddy, you can have a treat."

He would take it from their hands is such a gentle manner as to make sure his teeth never touched their skin. He took food from our hands like that from the first day we got him. I have no idea where he learned this. We were always curious as to his past.

When he would hear my keys rattle, he would be right behind me. He knew I was going somewhere, anywhere, and he wanted to go. However, he only wanted to go in the golf cart. That was his deal.

The golf cart was parked beside my truck in the garage, and he would immediately hop up in the back seat. If it was a short trip, I could take the golf cart, but sometimes I needed to take the truck. When I did, he would wait until I backed out of the garage and was about to leave the driveway before he would get out of the golf cart and come over to the truck. I guess he figured the truck was better than not getting to go at all.

He was such a cool dog that one time when the manager of our local grocery store was outside and saw Jill tie him up so she could go inside to get groceries, he went over to her and told her she could bring him inside to shop. She went up and down each aisle with her buggy while Buddy walked beside her.

He *loved* to go for walks on the beach. As usual, we would take a leash with us but rarely used it. We would leash him on the rare occasion when some other dog owner walking their dog would seem uncomfortable. Besides jumping in the waves, Buddy would walk right along beside us, minding his own business. Other dog owners were having to restrain their leashed dog with all their might.

Sometimes late in the evening before it got dark, he and I would take the golf cart to one of the back holes on the course. While I would chip and putt, he would sit on the green, watching me while patiently waiting. If anyone else came along, either walking, riding their bike, or in their golf cart, Buddy would chase them away, as if to say, "This is our green, go find your own." I would always yell at him to stop and apologize for his harmless behavior, and most would just laugh and go on. Buddy was a protector.

Another good story is when Buddy would see me pull up in the driveway, he would causally get up from his bench and slowly wander to the door to greet me. When he saw Jill pull up, he would spring off the bench, almost turning it over, and run to the door, often sliding on the hardwood floors with such speed he would crash into the walls, to greet her. He would jump up on her with such force he would knock the groceries from her hands. She would drop what she had and start loving on him. She wondered why he followed her around all day...

I have many, many stories about Buddy and even more great memories of him. He fell in love with Jill, and no matter how hard she tried not to, she fell head over heels right back in love with him. She was the nurturer, the one who would sit on the floor and pet him and rub his belly, feed him homemade meals instead of dog food, buy him more expensive treats than she bought me, and fret when we were gone from the house too long.

Buddy and I loved each other dearly, also. I was his caretaker, and he knew this. We loved each other in a different way, not in the roll-around-on-the-floor kind of way. I took him to the vet, kept up with his monthly meds and vaccines, washed and brushed him, made sure he was healthy, put in doggy doors and gates, kept his golf cart charged at all times, and made sure he was safe.

In the fall of our tenth year with him, he began to seem dizzy and was unable to keep his balance. He was lethargic, and going outside didn't interest him, which was unusual. After much testing and scans, he was diagnosed with an inoperable brain tumor.

We held on to hope that the medications he was given would bring some comfort and give him a few more months to live. We all, including our children and grandchildren, adored Buddy. We needed some time to wrap our brains around letting him go.

Within three weeks, we couldn't bear watching him suffer any longer. How could he have gone from being perfectly healthy, it seemed, to being so sick within such a short period of time? He could no longer eat, and he couldn't make it outside to do his business without falling. He was so embarrassed it seemed, almost ashamed.

I scheduled the euthanasia for the following Saturday morning.

We called the children to let them know, and some were able to visit him. Annabel came home from Nashville for a couple days to say goodbye. She was still in high school when we had brought him home in 2014, so he was a big part of her life, and he loved her as much as she loved him.

When the time came on Saturday, I had to physically lift him into the car to take him. At the vet's office, I held his head while they gave him a sedative to put him to sleep before administering the quick IV that would stop his heart. He felt nothing. He was at peace. He took his last breath, and I gently placed his head on the gurney and walked out the door.

No "Goodbye, Doc," no "Thank you, Doc" from me. I just walked out and left through the side door. Before it closed, I heard the doc say, "I'm sorry."

I made it to the parking lot before I lost it.

27

SELLING THE CLEVELAND DEALERSHIPS

In 2014, I began to confidentially consider selling the Cleveland dealerships. Selling Lenoir City Ford was not something we considered at the time. I knew our operator we had there wanted to work for another ten years or so, and it didn't require me being there. I had put in a lot of hours by the time I was fifty-eight years old, having been in the car business since I was eighteen.

No matter my positions over the years, including being a dealership owner, I usually worked six days a week. As an owner, I could work when I wanted, but I still worked full time and on Saturdays. I knew of many owners who didn't work even thirty hours a week. However, the harder I worked, the harder my employees worked. When they saw me there on Christmas Eve and New Year's Day, they didn't seem to mind being there, and they were more productive.

When they saw how important success was to me, it became more important to them. If I had to do it over again, I wouldn't change one thing, but it was time to step away from working full time. I wanted to start enjoying other things in life.

Much of the sales price you receive for a car dealership is "goodwill." *Goodwill* is what one is willing to pay to be the Ford dealer in a certain market. It's an intangible but can be the highest-priced piece of the deal. Goodwill value is based on the profitability of the business. The more money the business has made for the past several years, the higher goodwill one will pay. We had been doing extremely well, so the store would command a nice goodwill price.

A good time to sell is when you are ready to retire, and you can get a lot of money for your business. This seemed like a great time.

My CPA of twenty-plus years, Brent, is a super-smart guy. He was (and still is) a leader in his industry. He eats, sleeps, walks, and talks his trade. About the time I first met him, he had begun to specialize in automotive accounting, which is a different bird. It is very complex. A good car dealer doesn't find his or her CPA at H&R Block.

Brent had probably worked with fifty or more other CPAs over the years who also specialized in automotive accounting. These guys are all professionals and understand the seriousness of confidentiality in these matters, as I mentioned earlier in the book. I called Brent and told him I was considering selling if we could get the price I wanted for Larry Hill Ford and Larry Hill Imports.

Brent put together an impressive presentation detailing what we wanted for the stores and the financial documents to substantiate the price. He did a great job with it. Once I approved it, he confidentially contacted a few of the high-integrity CPAs he had worked with in the past. A car dealer's CPA knows if the dealer has interest in growing or downsizing and knows if his dealer has the money to buy another dealership. Brent knew that looking for a buyer through his CPA network was the safest and most confidential way to make a deal.

We knew the dealerships were very desirable, but both Brent and I predicted we would have one obstacle to overcome—the performance of my dealerships in a market of one-hundred thousand people was somewhat of an anomaly. It was very rare to find a business that generated this much income in a small market.

Much of our success was due to a marketing campaign I had installed ten years earlier that pulled buyers to us from outside our market. Not only did we sell a lot of vehicles in the Cleveland area, but as I mentioned before, we had also penetrated the Chattanooga market heavily and were selling a good number of vehicles in North Carolina and Georgia. Larry Hill Ford and Larry Hill Imports were forty miles from North Carolina and twenty-five miles from Georgia. Our marketing reached well into these areas.

However, we were still located in Bradley County, population one-hundred thousand. A potential buyer could easily say, "Hey, guys, before I spend this kind of money for a dealership in Cleveland, Tennessee, I'll look in larger markets such as Charlotte or Atlanta."

Brent had a dealer client in South Carolina who was aggressively acquiring dealerships and loved medium-sized markets. He owned six car dealerships that were all in markets similar to Cleveland. He understood these markets, was impressed with how well we performed, and wanted to come look at the stores.

I invited him to come see me on December 23, 2014. Brent flew up from Florida the evening before, and the prospective buyer and his CPA flew in the following morning. We visited in my office for a couple hours. They were very nice, professional men. No big egos at all. Just two genuine professionals.

After the meeting, they went back to South Carolina, and Brent flew back to Florida. Things were idle until after the holidays, and then Brent and the other CPA began the serious conversations. Several days later, we received a letter of intent signed by the prospective buyer.

Now came the months-long due-diligence process. It involved in-depth reviews of multiple years of financial statements, tax returns, performance reviews, customer satisfaction reports, sales effectiveness reports, inventories of assets, property appraisals, ground contamination inspections, and reports.

The buyer and I worked through the CPAs and lawyers to complete the deal. There were only a couple of items the teams couldn't agree on that required the buyer and me to personally converse. We hammered both out in pleasant fifteen-minute phone conversations. We closed the deal on

Larry Hill Ford and Larry Hill Imports on June 1, 2015. The closing took all day. We left the attorney's office about 5:00 p.m. on that Monday evening.

The next morning, I got up and had nowhere to go.

Chris, my right-hand guy and partner at Larry Hill Imports, retired when the stores sold. He's my age and had been doing it for as long as I had. I had known Chris for thirty years. We are still close today.

Fred and I still own Lenoir City Ford, but from a day-to-day perspective, I was unemployed.

On the Tuesday morning after the closing, I got busy preparing for a ten-day trip to Hawaii that Jill and I were going to take in a couple days. She left to run some errands and then called me at the house around 11:00 a.m. She was so upset and frantic that I couldn't understand what she was saying.

Once I got her calmed down, she explained that a niece called her to tell her that Whitfield and Sophia's dad had suddenly passed away. He had been sitting on the sofa in the living room of his home on Lookout Mountain a couple hours earlier, preparing for a golf tournament, and died of a massive heart attack. He was fifty-two years old. Man, what a blow. He had remarried and had three sons, all under fifteen years old. He left behind five children and a very nice stepson.

Naturally, we immediately cancelled our Hawaii plans and began offering whatever support we could to the family. This was an unbelievable tragedy. His children still mourn the loss of their dad and will forever, of course.

I think he would be very happy to see what fine adults they have become. They worked their way through the grief and are all very close. They are all doing well, have good jobs, and have made great lives for themselves.

Sophia inherited her dad's artistic gene of painting and earned a degree in art from college. We have a few of her beautiful paintings at our home. She went on to earn her master's in marriage and family counseling.

Whitfield inherited his dad's science and math gene, majoring in biochemistry and molecular biology. He earned an MBA at Belmont University a few years later and got a job with Caterpillar Finance. He is also creative and loves projects, designing and building things for his home.

Jill and I had decided after we retired, we would make our primary residence in Ponte Vedra Beach, Florida. We would keep a place in Chattanooga but would not need a home as big as what we had built a few years earlier.

We bought a home there and rented it out while we worked with an architect and builder on a remodel design.

Jill began to wind down her business, and I stayed busy doing a lot of things related to winding down Larry Hill Ford and Larry Hill Imports. Although the businesses had been sold, I still needed to close the old corporations. This was a very detailed process.

The buyer, per the contract, could keep my name on the businesses for three years, provided he continued to operate the stores in an ethical manner that mirrored how I ran them. He did, and after the three-year period was up, he renamed them Cleveland Ford and Cleveland Imports.

28

CHANGES AT LENOIR CITY FORD

The next year passed quickly. I had some time to take a deeper look into the best practices at Lenoir City Ford and try to figure out why it just didn't perform more in line with our standards.

I realized that Jim, our partner now of nine years, had just mentally pulled away from the day-to-day operations of the dealership. The first thing I took a good look at was to see if he was spending the proper amount of time at the store. He was there, he just wasn't leading. Jim was a good guy but had taken on more of a follower role than a leader role. As time went on, Fred and I had several strong heart-to-heart conversations with him, but he continued to underperform. Jim's biggest weakness was the way he ran the Sales Department—the key department in any car dealership. You have to sell the car first.

I knew a great car guy in Florida whom I had hired when I ran the Toyota Olds dealership in Daytona Beach. His name is Glenn Wood. Glenn is the one who owned the condo in Daytona Beach where Gayle, the girls, and I stayed on vacation, which I mentioned earlier in the book. I had hired him in 1988, and he worked for me for twelve years. I gave him multiple promotions, and he rose to the challenge with each one. Later in his career, he worked for my partner, Fred, when he still owned his dealership. He worked for Fred for only about a year, but that was long enough for Fred to know he was a good car guy.

When I left Florida to go to Cleveland, Glenn went to work as the General Manager for a Ford dealer in Melbourne, Florida. Glenn did a great job there. Although I was in Cleveland and Glenn was in Melbourne, we talked a couple times a month for years. We were and still are very close. Glenn and Cathy raised two great kids. Justin had graduated from college and was well into his career, and Brooke was in college. Glenn and Cathy were empty-nesters and were considering a move. They had been in Florida most of their lives and were a little tired of the constant heat, no seasons, etc. Glenn had expressed a desire to possibly relocate to a more favorable climate like Tennessee. Glenn and our partner at Lenoir City Ford, Jim, knew each other as well. They both had run dealerships in Florida about twenty miles apart before I had hired Jim in 2008. They had become acquaintances and maybe even friends. Jim knew that Glenn was a good car guy.

I knew Jim's weakness was Glenn's strength, so I suggested to Jim that we hire Glenn as his General Sales Manager for the dealership. Although it was one job level below what Glenn had been doing, once we discussed it, he accepted the position.

I should have stopped right there and realized I was working too hard to save Jim's job. I have been guilty in the past of working too hard to save an employee. If I ever had to terminate an employee, he or she knew it was coming. I gave people too much help and too much warning for them to be surprised when I had to terminate them. If I had to terminate someone for an honesty or integrity issue, I'd cut their legs out from under them so quickly they would never know it was coming. Other than that, I gave plenty of chances.

Jim sure didn't have integrity or honesty issues; however, after all the assistance I had given him, to no avail, looking back, I should have terminated him when I hired Glenn.

When we brought in Glenn as the General Sales Manager, Jim still would not hand the reins of the Sales Department over to Glenn. After ninety or so days of working with him and persuading him, Fred and I decided it was time to buy him out of his partnership. Jim had been our partner for nine years, so this was a difficult decision. We had our CPA calculate the stock value of the business, and we bought Jim's stock back. Fred wrote him a check for half, and I wrote him a check for half.

I was very frustrated. Had Jim not told me he wanted to work for another ten or so years, I would have sold Lenoir City Ford to the buyer of the two Cleveland dealerships.

He would have loved the whole package. He was in an aggressive growth mode, and the size and demographics of Lenoir City matched his model well. And, if we hadn't just moved Glenn and his wife to Lenoir City, and they hadn't settled into a new home, we still would have considered putting the dealership on the market to sell.

After parting ways with Jim, we offered Glenn the opportunity to manage the store for us, and we'd see how it worked out. He was excited for the opportunity. Glenn accepted the challenge with the zeal of an operator twenty years his junior. He was hungry to show us we had made the right decision. From the outside looking in, the place seemed OK when Glenn took the reins. There were no employee or customer issues.

I began going to the dealership for two or three days at a time to help get us back on track. Each time I returned, I could see the wonderful progress Glenn was making. After each visit, I knew more and more that we had made the right decision. After about two years, my visits dropped to one day a month. That is still what I do today. If we are in Tennessee, I drive up, as it's only an hour and a half ride from our house. If we are in Florida, I fly there, and Glenn picks me up at the airport. We have dinner and a couple cocktails and laugh about the old days in Daytona, when we were twenty-five and thirty years old. He drops me off afterward at the hotel, he picks me up the next morning, and we spend the day at the dealership. I leave later that day and fly back to Florida. Not a bad gig.

29

FINALLY SETTLING INTO RETIREMENT

Jill and I have established a bit of a schedule where we spend the hot summer months on Lookout Mountain, Tennessee, and then head back to Ponte Vedra Beach for the winter.

In addition to the cooler summer temperatures, Lookout is covered with huge, mature trees that provide a lot of shade. The summers are comfortable on the mountain.

It is a great place. It is very laid back, and you do feel as though you stepped back in time when you are up there. Lookout Mountain continues to run well into Georgia. The population of Lookout Mountain, Tennessee is about two thousand, with around seven-hundred and seventy households. Although the top of the mountain is only a 10-to-12-minute drive to downtown Chattanooga, the weather, especially fog and some winter snow, can make the drive a challenge at times.

We have just about everything we need on the mountain. There is a small area I refer to as "downtown" that has a nice casual restaurant, a post office, a coffee shop, a great little food market, a gas station where they still pump your gas and do mechanical repairs, and a bank. We even have a wine and spirits store. The Lookout Mountain Police staff are the nicest police officers you have ever met anywhere. I'm sure their firearms only come out of their holsters for routine required shooting practice and training.

We go back to Ponte Vedra each October. Ponte Vedra Beach is a great small town on the Atlantic coast about twenty-five minutes from downtown Jacksonville, Florida. We live in an area called "Old Ponte Vedra" behind the Ponte Vedra Inn and Club. Our house is three blocks from the beach. The club has wonderful amenities: golf, tennis, a spa, a fitness center, retail shopping, great cafés and restaurants, a beach club, pools, etc. All are a short golf-cart ride from the house. Golf carts are street-legal in Ponte Vedra, so we use ours as a regular mode of transportation.

Since we are in North Florida, we do experience a bit of the seasons, which is nice; however, you can easily play golf with little more than a couple of layers on in the winter. Beginning around mid-June, it begins to get very hot. This is when we head back up to Lookout.

Annabel graduated from Auburn in 2019. She had worked for two years while in school and all summer the year between her junior and senior year, studying for the dental school acceptance test. She aced the test and had one of the highest scores recorded in the United States for that year's entries, and then she was accepted to the University of Tennessee Health & Science program. Her dad, Tommy, Jill, and I moved her to Memphis to begin dental school.

I had met Tommy a few times at graduations, weddings, and other family functions that bring separated families together. He had always been very cordial, and I enjoyed visiting with him from time to time at these various functions.

He was a retired dentist and had been diagnosed with cancer when Annabel was a young child but had been in remission for eighteen years. During her very short summer break between her second and third years of dental school, his cancer returned. His condition worsened quickly.

Tommy knew that Annabel and I had mutual respect and trust. One day, he called and asked if I would stop by his house, which was about five minutes from ours on Lookout. We visited for an hour probably. He was in immense pain. He asked me to look at his will and asked if I would help Annabel with his estate when he passed. I agreed.

After that, he and I would spend a few minutes most days reviewing how he wanted things done. Annabel was his only child, and he had been very generous and responsible with how he left things for her.

Whitfield brought Caroline, his then-girlfriend, over a few times, introducing her to Tommy and visiting. Sophia also came many times and sat by his side, holding his hand to help bring him peace.

Annabel stayed with him every day when she was home from school. She didn't leave his side. Toward the end, she stayed full-time and would make up classes and clinics later.

Although I disagree, Jill has always said she had not been available for Whitfield and Sophia when their dad passed and still says she will never get over the guilt of this. She knew she needed to be there during that time for Annabel, so she and I would make it a point to spend as much time there as we could. She and Annabel were holding hands and praying over Tommy when he passed peacefully in his sleep in the early evening of September 3, 2021. He was sixty-four years old. Now all three of Jill's children were left without a dad.

Annabel briefly considered taking a leave from school to grieve her loss but knew her dad would want her to get back to school. He had specifically told her this.

So she headed back to face her two toughest years. She had two professors who were the clinic group leaders in her small dental group at school. One had lost her parents while she was in dental school, and the other professor had lost his father in dental school and then later his only child. They understood grief and were a huge support for her during this tough period. We will always be grateful to them for their kindness.

EPILOGUE

All continues to move along smoothly with the family. We are beyond blessed. The kids and grandkids are doing well and are very busy just living life.

Emily, my youngest, married Jordan, a nice young man she met in Nashville. They gave us our first grandchild, Luca Ernest Brunelle, born on November 22, 2017. My family says Luca is my mini-me. He walks, talks, and looks like me when I was a child, and he has my exact mannerisms. When we're together, he is my shadow, following me around, asking "Pop" questions constantly.

Allison married Bennett, a nice young man she met while at Belmont University. Allison and Bennett decided to go the childless route. I jokingly tell them they are the smartest in the group. Ha.

Sophia married Wesley, a nice young man she met in Chattanooga. Shortly after came their two children—Judah on December 12, 2018, and Violet on June 12, 2020. Two of the cutest kids you've ever seen. Judah is the sweet, older brother who takes care of his younger sister, and Violet is a total boss.

Then soon afterward, Emily and Jordan brought us Genevieve, Luca's little sister, on November 24, 2020. Luca is also the sweet older brother, and Genevieve is the boss as well.

Thankfully, both boys don't mind at all, and they think their sisters hung the moon.

The following spring, in 2022, Whitfield and Caroline were married at a neat ceremony in Sewanee, Tennessee, where Caroline had graduated college. They announced in the winter of 2022 that they were expecting twin boys! Leo and Theo were born in August 2023. They relocated to Lookout Mountain, about five minutes from our house. Caroline works remotely for Caterpillar Finance, and Whitfield accepted a job in commercial insurance sales with a local family-owned insurance business in Chattanooga.

Annabel is in a serious relationship with a wonderful young man, Jason, whom she met in dental school. They both graduated with their DDS degrees in May 2023. He is from Signal Mountain, another suburb of Chattanooga, but ironically, their paths never crossed until they were both in Memphis. Jason is from a great family. No doubt he was her rock as she went through those last two years of dental school.

She is now practicing in Nashville, and Jason is in a residency in Little Rock. He was accepted into the pediatric dentistry program at LSU and will begin there in the summer of 2024 for a two-year program.

Linda is still going wide open at With Love From Jesus. It's amazing how much energy she has. Slowing down isn't on her radar.

Glenn and his team at the dealership continue to do a great job. We talk and exchange emails a couple times a week. I enjoy my monthly visits to Lenoir City Ford.

Jill and I both love the two places where we have settled. Much of the family are able to make it to Ponte Vedra once or twice during the year for a beach vacation.

In between, Jill and I try to work in a couple of fun trips together. We recently bought a Sprinter Van for road travel. It has nice big seats and a sofa for naps. Jill has a nice TV in it for SEC football games while we are cruising down the road. We did our maiden shakedown trip up to the New England area a few months ago. All went well. We plan to travel some more in it.

Jill *loves* being a grandmother. The more the better for her. I've never seen a woman who enjoys it as much as her. She will go from Ponte Vedra to Lookout Mountain (a 7.5-hour drive) just to keep some of the grandkids for a day or two. Now she has four grandchildren within twenty minutes of our Lookout home. Two more grandchildren are only two hours away in Columbia, Tennessee, near Nashville.

Something tells me that Jill's "primary residence" may become Lookout Mountain. I like to kid her by saying, "You can find me in Ponte Vedra Beach."

ACKNOWLEDGMENTS

If not for several great friends and the influence of many, this book would not have been written. I could write pages of thanks to the many people who have been a great influence on me during my sixty-eight years. However, there are several who played a huge role in bringing this book to print and who made my life easier. I would like to acknowledge them.

Michelle Hill: Michelle and her Winning Proof team coordinated this book from concept to print. They held my hand every step of the way. Great work!

Libbye Morris: Libbye of Legacy Ghostwriter, LLC, wrote the book. While I authored it, Libbye placed the words on the pages. Her knowledge and experience in this arena are second to none.

My parents: Ernest and Rometa Hill. Regardless of the good or the bad, I wouldn't be here today if not for them. They did the absolute best they could with the tools they had.

Dennis Higginbotham: My life could have gone in so many directions if not for Dennis. When we met, I was a broke autobody repair technician looking for a job so I could spend a few more months in Florida. I can't thank Dennis enough for the opportunities he offered me over the span of twenty-plus years.

Hayden Byrd: Hayden took me under his wing while I was trying to figure out life at the young age of twenty-one. He mentored me for twenty years. He has been a wonderful friend. Everyone needs a Hayden Byrd in their life.

Raleigh Geddings: Raleigh was my right-hand man when I opened the doors at Larry Hill Ford on November 1, 2003. It took every bit of the horsepower he and I both had to get the place out of the ditch. I could not have done it without him.

Fred Bondesen: Fred and I have been friends for twenty-plus years. He was quick to agree to join me as an investor when I started Larry Hill Ford. Fred and I are still partners in Lenoir City Ford. I have enjoyed our business and personal relationship. I couldn't ask for a better partner.

Barbara Middlebrooks: Barbara was the Controller at the previous dealership that became Larry Hill Ford. She was just one of four employees who were there when I bought the store and was still there when I sold it. Barbara still works for us today as the Controller at Lenoir City Ford. Barbara is the best. Twenty great years!

Randy Tomlinson: Randy worked at the dealership when I bought it, as did Barbara. He was there the day I sold it. Randy was the most trusted employee I have ever known. The car business requires a lot of hours away from home. I had little time to handle personal things, including sometimes picking up Emily at school after her mom and

I divorced. Randy was the best when it came to keeping my business private. He had keys to the dealerships and my home. He was available 24/7 for anything I needed. He managed all this while still managing a department of ten employees. At some time, I think he moved every one of our five kids to or from college. They all knew him as a family member.

Glenn Wood: I hired Glenn when he was twenty-five years old. He just turned sixty-one and runs the dealership in Lenoir City. He is an outstanding car guy, and more importantly a great friend. If you need to laugh yourself sick, call Glenn. *They only made one Glenn Wood.*

Linda Williams: My sister, Linda, and I are the only ones left from our original immediate family. I know Linda prays for me regularly. I know her prayers have contributed greatly to my success.

Lee Stewart: I met Lee a month before I moved to Cleveland, Tennessee, while opening a business account with his bank. He was president of Southern Heritage Bank. Cleveland is a conservative town. Most were skeptical of a car guy who blew in from Florida. When I needed something, I called Lee. No vice president or clerk. He would pick up the phone and give me whatever I needed. Man, those were the good old days of solid relationships.

Robert Thompson: Robert is a very successful attorney and real estate investor in Cleveland. Robert may be the most well-known person in Cleveland. It was tough breaking into this very tight-knit community. He befriended me soon after I arrived. It makes breaking into a community like

Cleveland much easier when you have Robert Thompson running interference for you. We are still great friends today.

Wes Robbins: Shortly after arriving in Cleveland, Wes and I became workout partners at a small private gym that Robert owned. He is a great Certified Financial Planner® and real estate investor, but a better friend. We talk weekly. Wes is the vault. I can tell him anything, and I know it goes nowhere. I don't care how many friends one may have. They probably don't have a Wes.

Chris Sather: Chris was my partner at Larry Hill Imports and managed the Sales and Finance Departments for both Larry Hill Ford and Larry Hill Imports. One of the best car guys walking the planet. Much of our success was due to Chris's hard work and commitment to me. Thanks, Chris!

Randy Johnson: Randy was the best Service and Parts Director I have ever known. A true visionary. He worked for me for eight years and sure made me look good. He went on to start and build Car People Marketing, a national automotive service marketing and customer retention company based in Daytona Beach. His company recently celebrated its twenty-year anniversary. Randy and I have remained great friends.

My Monday-Night Men's Group Warriors: To keep with the spirit and integrity of confidentiality that we all agreed to, I will not mention last names: **Ron** (El Jefe), **Vic, Peter, Sam, Bill, Brian, Bob, Sean, Fred, Todd, Gary.** Thanks for all you guys did to keep me between the ditches.

Larry Hill

www.ingramcontent.com/pod-product-compliance
Lightning Source LLC
Chambersburg PA
CBHW062150080426
42734CB00010B/1633